MAKE AND TAKES
FOR KIDS

MAKE AND TAKES FOR KIDS

50 crafts throughout the year

Marie LeBaron

WILEY

John Wiley & Sons, Inc.

Published by John Wiley & Sons, Inc., Hoboken, New Jersey
Published simultaneously in Canada

For general information on our other products and services or to obtain technical support please contact our Customer Care Department within the U.S. at (877) 762-2974, outside the U.S. at (317) 572-3993 or fax (317) 572-4002.

John Wiley & Sons, Inc. also publishes its books in a variety of electronic formats and by print-on-demand. Not all content that is available in standard print versions of this book may appear or be packaged in all book formats. If you have purchased a version of this book that did not include media that is referenced by or accompanies a standard print version, you may request this media by visiting http://booksupport.wiley.com. For more information about Wiley products, visit us at www.wiley.com.

Library of Congress Control Number: 2011936908
ISBN: 978-1-118-08336-9 (pbk)
ISBN: 978-1-118-15992-7; 978-1-118-18321-2; 978-1-118-18320-5 (ebk)

Printed in the United States of America

10   9   8   7   6   5   4   3   2   1

Book production by John Wiley & Sons, Inc. Composition Services

CREDITS

Senior Editor
Roxane Cerda

Project Editor
Carol Pogoni

Editorial Manager
Christina Stambaugh

Vice President and Publisher
Cindy Kitchel

Vice President and Executive Publisher
Kathy Nebenhaus

Interior Design
Erin Zeltner

Cover Design
Jose Almaguer

Photography
Nicole Hill Gerulat

**Wardrobe and
Prop Styling**
Mallory Ullman

Photo Assistants
Kailee Higgins and Jordyn Hill

Illustrations
Melissa Smith

For Matthew, Lucy, and Anna

ACKNOWLEDGMENTS

Thank you to Roxane, Cindy, and Carol at Wiley for your support and guidance to make this book a reality. Thank you to Nicole for her amazing photography, which make my crafts come to life. Thank you to Make and Takes blog readers for their loyalty and encouragement. Thank you to all the educators in my life who made learning fun; you planted the seed in me to becoming a teacher myself, especially Mrs. Floor who had such creative holiday projects.

I want to thank my husband, Jordan, for always supporting me and my crafty endeavors. Thank you to my children Matthew, Lucy, and Anna for being my creative inspiration.Thank you to my family and friends, who have believed and supported me through this journey.

TABLE OF

CONTENTS

JULY

AUGUST

SEPTEMBER

OCTOBER

NOVEMBER

DECEMBER

CRAFTING OVERVIEW

The reasons to craft with your children are virtually

endless: discovery, wonder, exploration, creativity,

learning, bonding, and the simple gift of your time. The

projects in *Make and Takes for Kids* are unique but

simple to produce, so all parents, educators, caregivers,

and children can easily make them. Each craft requires

little preparation and only a few supplies (discussed in

the next chapter), which you can readily find at a local

craft-supply store or even at home. With only a minimal

investment, you will be well on your way to creating

quality time by crafting together as a family.

Make and Takes for Kids contains 50 crafts to create all year long. It's all about crafts, food, and fun, which is my motto over at my personal blog, Make and Takes (www.makeandtakes.com). Whether you're looking for a winter day activity, a treat for Valentine's Day, or a spooky-eye card for Halloween, this book includes all kinds of holiday- and seasonal-inspired projects that will get you crafting and creating with your children throughout the year.

The crafts and activities are organized by calendar month and include 3–4 mainstream holidays as well as seasonal projects. For each month, there are 3–4 crafts and at least 1 food project. I love to work with kids in the kitchen, so I've included some activities where you can create with food.

Many projects can be reused in different colors for a different holiday, or you can tailor a project to your customs and culture. For example, you can swap out the buttons from the Flag Button Card with the colors of the Irish flag to celebrate St. Patrick's Day instead of the Fourth of July.

This book also includes several crafts that are eco-friendly. This is a great way to encourage children to reuse and recycle materials already found at home, while teaching children about frugality.

LEARNING OBJECTIVES

Crafting isn't just about playtime; all of the gluing, cutting, and coloring serve an educational purpose as well. Children are learning hand-eye coordination, fine motor skills, problem solving, math, teamwork, and individual expression. They are exercising creativity and enhancing their imaginations. *Make and Takes for Kids* provides ideas and activities that enhance learning. While making a project together, you can determine your child's strengths and weaknesses. You can also praise your child's improvement in a skill after he or she completes a project.

In this book, the learning objectives are stated at the beginning of each activity to let you know what types of skills your child might learn from making a craft project. (For more information, please refer to the "Learning while Crafting: A Learning Objectives Overview" at the back of this book.) It may take your child a few tries to master a skill, but keep in mind that this is a learning process. These projects also reinforce educational assessment and emphasize that crafting with kids has a lasting impact by teaching skills that children will use throughout their lifetime.

THE CREATIVE PROCESS

Crafting with your child is not always about the end result. It is more about the *process* of how a child gets there. Don't worry if the craft doesn't come out looking perfect or doesn't look like the one in the book. The creative process itself is the most important component when crafting with your children. Feel free to let your child discover a different way to create each craft or add something new to the project. I hope you can use this book as a stepping-stone to you and your child becoming more creative.

BASIC SUPPLIES

This basic supply list will get you through most of

the crafts in this book. You can find everything you

need at a local craft store, in your recycling bin, or

at your grocery store. *NOTE: A few supplies are*

recommended for adults only and are listed on the

following pages.

- **Beads:** I used plastic "pony" beads for all the projects that require beads in this book. Pony beads are a type of plastic bead that have large holes for threading yarn or pipe cleaners. I recommend purchasing a large bag of colorful beads in order to save money.

- **Crayons, colored pencils, and markers:** For most projects, these three coloring options are interchangeable.

- **Glue:** You can find all three glue types listed below at most craft stores.

    Craft Glue: I recommend using white craft glue for most of the projects in this book. You can find it in craft stores, it's non-toxic and safe for children to use, and you should be able to get you through all 50 crafts in this book with only 1–2 bottles of glue. However, if you already have another type of glue on hand, the following types of glue will also work for most of the projects in this book: glue sticks, glue dots, spray glue, school glue, and tacky glue.

    Decoupage Glue: At least one project requires the use of decoupage glue.

    Hot Glue and Gun: A couple of projects call for hot glue and a glue gun, which are adult use only.

- **Paint:** You should use basic acrylic craft paint for each project that requires paint, but the supply list will simply list "craft paint" throughout the book. Acrylic craft paint is a non-toxic paint and it works well with all the projects in this book. Make sure you protect hard surfaces with a paper plate, newspaper, or paper towel when using craft paint for a project. (Note: The only exception to this is for the April Coffee Filter Umbrella project, in which you use watercolor paints.)

- **Paintbrush:** I recommend a 1"-wide sponge brush for every painting project in this book, but you can use a basic watercolor paintbrush if you prefer.

- **Paper:** Each project specifies what type of paper you will need. If a project calls for craft paper, then you can use art paper, construction paper, scrapbook paper, or colored printer paper. Projects that need a heavier paper will specifically call for cardstock paper in the supply list. The basic paper size for most projects is 8½ × 11", but you can use a larger size, such as 12 × 12" scrapbook paper, if that is what you have on hand.

- **Scissors:** You need both adult and child-size scissors. Most of the projects allow for children to do the cutting. If you have a younger child or a child who is not quite capable of using scissors, then you may need to evaluate whether you need to do the cutting for a particular project.

- **Basic craft items:** For the following items, I have specified the size or length requirements for each item within each project. But you are welcome to improvise by using items that you already have on hand from previous craft projects or from supplies you purchased in bulk at a discounted price.

Buttons	Pom-poms, store-bought or handmade (you can find pom-pom making tools at most craft stores)
Craft foam	
Glitter	
Googly eyes, also sold as "wiggle eyes" or "plastic craft eyes"	Ribbon
	Sewing elastic
Hole punch	Smooth polystyrene foam
Ink pad	Tissue paper
Letter stickers	Wooden board
Pipe cleaners, also sold as "chenille stems" or "fuzzy sticks"	Wooden dowel
	Yarn

◆ **Recycled Items:**

Bubble wrap

Cereal boxes

Cube-shaped tissue boxes

Egg cartons

Glass bottles

Paper towel rolls

Plastic gallon-size milk jugs

Water bottles

◆ **Household/Yard Items:**

Apples

Birdseed

Coffee filters

Clothespins

Drinking straws

Headband

Knit winter hat and gloves

Leaves

Pinecones

Rocks

Shower curtain rings

◆ **Kitchen and Grocery Items:** Specific quantities of these items are listed in each project's supply list.

Berries

Bowls

Breadsticks, both store-bought
    breadstick dough and store-bought
    hard pre-packaged breadsticks

Butter

Candy-coated chocolate candies

Candy corn

Cereal

Chocolate chips

Chocolate wafer or sandwich cookies

Corncobs

Cupcakes (store-bought or homemade)

Cups

Eggshells from hardboiled eggs

Food coloring

Frosting (store-bought or homemade)

Gumdrop candies

Knife

Licorice

Lollipop sticks

Marshmallows

Meatballs

Raisins

Spoon

Sugar

Sugar cookie dough (store-bought or
    homemade)

Vanilla ice cream

White baking chocolate

JANUARY

With the frosty chill of winter, it's time to get cozy and craft. Stay warm wearing a silly snow-bug hat and animal-inspired winter gloves or sip on a snowman smoothie while you craft a winter wonderland puzzle.

Winter Glove
Animal Puppets

WINTER GLOVE ANIMAL PUPPETS

These furry little creatures come to life with knit gloves. Kids can pretend to take these cute animal puppets out to the pond or into the forest for a fun adventure.

Learning Objectives: Children will learn about animals; children will engage in pretend play with these puppets.

SUPPLIES

1 white knit glove, any size
1 pink knit glove, any size
1 green knit glove, any size
1 sheet pink craft foam
1 sheet green craft foam
1 small pink pom-pom
1 red pipe cleaner
½" piece of black paper or black pipe cleaner
6 medium-size googly eyes
Black permanent marker
Craft glue
Scissors

STEPS

Bunny: With the white glove, fold the thumb, first, and fifth glove fingers back into the glove. Cut 2 pink ears from the pink craft foam; as shown in the photo, these should be slightly smaller and in the same outline as a glove finger. Glue the ears onto the 2 remaining glove fingers. Glue 2 googly eyes and a pink pom-pom nose on the center of the glove. Draw the bunny's mouth with your black marker.

Frog: With the green glove, fold the middle glove finger back into the glove. Glue 2 googly eyes on the center of the glove, just below the middle finger. Fold the red pipe cleaner in half and twist it around itself. (Alternatively, you can just cut a pipe cleaner in half and skip the twisting part.) Slide the twisted red pipe cleaner into the hole left by the folded-in middle finger; this represents the frog's tongue. You can also curl a ½" piece of black pipe cleaner into a ball or use a small piece of black paper and attach it to the end of the red pipe cleaner tongue so it looks like the frog has caught a fly. Cut out 4 small ½"-circumference circles out of the green craft foam. Glue them onto the glove, as shown in the photo, to represent spots on the frog's back.

Pig: With the pink glove, fold the thumb, third, and fifth glove fingers back into the glove. Cut out a small pink oval shape (about 1" wide) from the pink craft foam. This shape represents the pig's nose. Draw 2 small black ovals onto the pink craft foam and color them in so they look like the pig's nostrils. Glue the pink oval shape onto the center of the glove to represent the pig's nose. Glue 2 googly eyes above the pink nose, as shown in the photo. Draw a mouth below the nose with your black marker. For the pig's floppy ears, bend down each remaining glove finger at a right-degree angle and glue in place.

Place these animal puppets onto your kid's hands and they can go on an adventure.

Snowman Smoothie

SNOWMAN SMOOTHIE

Let your kids build a snowman inside your house by creating this snowman smoothie. Have fun making your snowman come to life with these tasty ingredients.

Learning Objectives: Children will use math and measuring skills as they prepare their smoothie; children will work on creativity as they decorate the snowman's face.

SUPPLIES

16 oz. clear drinking glass
2 cups vanilla ice cream
½ cup milk
Blender
3 chocolate cookies
1 orange-colored bendy straw
8" piece of red ribbon, any width

STEPS

1. In a blender, mix up 2 cups of vanilla ice cream with ½ cup of milk until it has a creamy smooth consistency. (Note: You want to make sure the smoothie is thick enough that the cookies will stay on top and not sink in.)

2. Pour the ice cream mix into your clear drinking glass.

3. Break up your chocolate cookies into small pieces. Add them to the top of the smoothie to make a snowman face; use 2 pieces for the eyes and 6–7 cookie pieces to make a smile.

4. Place an orange straw in the center of your glass for the snowman's nose. A bendy straw works best because you can bend it outwards like a carrot nose.

5. Tie the red ribbon around your glass in a knot to create the snowman's scarf, placing it about 2" away from the top of the glass.

This smoothie makes for a tasty treat on a cold, wintry day!

Snow-Bug Hat

SNOW-BUG HAT

Your child can explore life as a bug as he or she becomes one with this fun and silly bug hat. Your child will crawl, fly, and sneak into all sorts of fun during playtime.

Learning Objectives: Children will dress up and use their imagination as they pretend play; children will use their creativity as they make a silly bug; children will use science skills as they discover the characteristics of an insect.

SUPPLIES

Knit hat (in your child's size), any color

2 pipe cleaners, any color

Hot glue (adults only) or craft glue

Large plastic pony beads

Buttons, variety of sizes and colors (optional)

Pom-poms (optional)

Googly eyes (optional)

STEPS

1. First you will make the bug's antennae. Insert a pipe cleaner through your knit hat, about an inch away from the center. Make sure you leave the long end of the pipe cleaner sticking out of the top of the hat. On the inside of the hat, twist the end of the pipe cleaner into a small circle to secure it. Repeat with another pipe cleaner, inserting it approximately 2–3" away from the first pipe cleaner (and an inch away from the center of the hat).

2. Attach beads or buttons to each of the long pipe cleaners if you want to add a fun texture or element. You can form each of the pipe cleaners into a corkscrew or zigzag so it looks like an insect's antenna. You can also form a small circle or curl at the top of the pipe cleaner antennae, which will help to hold the beads and buttons in place.

3. Using hot glue (adults only) or craft glue, add any other embellishments that you like to the hat, such as pre-made pom-poms from the craft store, googly eyes, and so on.

Now the hat is ready to wear and your child can buzz all around town.

Winter Wonderland
Cereal Box Puzzle

WINTER WONDERLAND CEREAL BOX PUZZLE

Your child will have fun creating this winter wonderland puzzle as he or she draws the image, cuts out each puzzle piece, and puts it all back together. This is the perfect activity to do together with your child on a cold winter night as you sit next to a fire and drink hot cocoa together.

Learning Objectives: Children will learn creativity as they color their picture; children will learn about the season of winter; children will help the environment by reusing and recycling craft supplies.

SUPPLIES

Empty cereal box
Scissors
White craft paint
Craft paint, variety of other colors
Paintbrush
Pencil

STEPS

1. Using your scissors, cut out one large rectangular side from an empty cereal box. Try to make each side as straight as possible.
2. With your paint and brush, paint the inside of the rectangle white. Let this dry completely.
3. Once the white paint is dry, use a pencil to draw a fun wintry scene onto the cereal box piece. (Or you can skip this part and go straight to step #4.)
4. With your paints and brushes, color a winter wonderland picture. You can paint a winter scene with snow, mountains, and trees; or paint just a snowman. Let the picture dry overnight.
5. On the back of the picture, draw puzzle shapes with your pencil. You can make your puzzle pieces any size or shape. Make sure each piece connects to the next so you can find and put them together later.
6. With your scissors, cut out each piece of the puzzle on the pencil lines.

Now turn each piece over and put together your new puzzle.

FEBRUARY

February is all about hearts as you and your

kids spread the love with crafts. Create all

kinds of heart-shaped projects and share

them with your Valentine.

Foam Heart
Friendship Bracelet

FOAM HEART FRIENDSHIP BRACELET

Show off and share this cute heart-shaped bracelet. It's the perfect gift to give a friend for Valentine's Day or any time of the year.

Learning Objectives: Children will learn fine motor skills as they weave yarn through holes in each foam heart; children will learn to recognize the shape of a heart; children will better understand the meaning of friendship as they create a bracelet for a friend.

SUPPLIES

Craft foam sheets in red, pink, and/or white

9–10" of yarn, any color

Hole punch

Scissors

Tape (optional)

Rhinestone stickers (optional)

Glitter glue (optional)

STEPS

1. Using your scissors, cut out 6–7 small 1 × 1" hearts from the craft foam sheets. You will need 6–7 hearts per child, although the length of the bracelet may vary for each child.

2. Use your hole punch to make 2 holes in each heart, as shown in the photo. You may have to press hard with your hole punch to get through the craft foam.

3. Wrap a small piece of tape around one end of your piece of yarn to help with lacing each heart and to prevent the yarn from fraying.

4. Lace the yarn through the foam hearts, weaving in and out of each hole. Lace up as many hearts as you need to fit the bracelet around your child's wrist.

5. Once all the hearts are on the yarn, tie the two ends of the yarn together in a knot and trim the ends. Make sure you tie the bracelet so that it is big enough for your child to take on and off easily.

You can add a few rhinestone stickers or glitter glue to the tops of the hearts to glitz them up or simply keep them as is. Now this bracelet is ready to give to a friend or loved one.

Heart-Shaped
Pretzel Bread

HEART-SHAPED PRETZEL BREAD

Rolling and shaping dough is the perfect activity for kids to help with in the kitchen. These hearts are simple for small hands to shape. Adding a little pink salt on top makes it all the more fun!

Learning Objectives: Children will learn the shape of a heart; children will use fine motor skills as they shape the dough with their fingers.

SUPPLIES

1 package store-bought breadstick dough

Baking pan

Salt, coarse or Kosher salt works best

Salt shaker or a bowl and spoon

Red food coloring

STEPS

1. Preheat the oven to the temperature listed on the dough package (or recipe if you choose to make your own dough).

2. Take a piece of breadstick dough and roll it into a long snakelike piece, about ½" thick. Form the dough into a heart shape, pressing the two ends together when they meet. Repeat for all the remaining breadstick dough and place the heart shapes onto a lined or greased baking pan.

3. In a small bowl or salt shaker, add 1 tbsp. of salt. Add 1–2 drops of red food coloring to the salt and mix or shake it together. Your salt will start to turn pink as you mix it together.

4. Shake or spoon the salt onto your heart-shaped dough, covering the entire top of each heart. You can gently press the salt into the dough to help it stick.

5. Bake the dough according to the directions on the dough recipe or package.

Once the heart bread cools slightly after baking, enjoy some yummy pink-salted pretzel bread that will warm your heart.

Lovely Heart
Bookmark

LOVELY HEART BOOKMARK

If you have a love of books, then you'll love this heart-shaped bookmark. It's also a great gift for a child to make for a loved one on Valentine's Day.

Learning Objectives: Children will use their fine motor skills as they cut out each heart shape; children will learn the shape of a heart.

SUPPLIES

1 sheet red craft paper
1 sheet white craft paper
1 sheet pink craft paper
Pencil
Scissors
Craft glue
Hole punch
1 sheet black letter stickers
3" piece of red ribbon, any width

STEPS

1. With your pencil, draw six 2 × 2" hearts from the craft paper, 2 from each color. Cut out each of the paper hearts.

2. Put a small dab of glue on the bottom of one heart and attach it to the top of a second heart, as shown in the photo. Repeat this process until all 6 of your hearts are glued together in a line.

3. With your hole punch, make a hole at the top of the line of hearts in the center.

4. Thread your ribbon through the hole and tie it off in a knot, as shown in the photo.

5. You can make your bookmark a little extra special by using black letter stickers to spell out the word "LOVE" on top of the paper hearts.

6. To add a little extra love to this bookmark, you could glue a photo or two of a loved one onto the hearts.

This bookmark is now ready to save your place in a storybook that you love.

Ribboned Heart
Doorknob Hanger

RIBBONED HEART DOORKNOB HANGER

Make several ribbon-wrapped hearts and hang them all around your house to set the mood for Valentine's Day. There will be lots of love to go around with these bright spots of pink.

Learning Objectives: Children will use their fine motor skills as they wrap this doorknob hanger; children will develop shape recognition of a heart.

SUPPLIES

Empty cereal box
Pencil
Scissors
10' of pink ribbon, ⅝" width
    (per heart)
Hole punch (optional)
Craft glue

STEPS

1. With your scissors, cut out 1 of the largest rectangular sides of your empty cereal box. (You will need 1 rectangle for each heart you make.)

2. Using the photo as a guide, draw the shape of a 5–6"-wide heart on one of the cardboard cutouts. Draw a smaller heart inside the larger one, starting about 1" away from the larger heart. (Your heart will be about 1" thick all the way around.)

3. Using your scissors, cut out the larger heart by following the pencil line. To cut out the inside of the heart, you can fold the heart in half slightly to start the cutting or you can use a hole punch to create a small opening where you can begin to cut.

4. Glue one end of your ribbon to one side of your cardboard heart. Then begin to wrap the ribbon around and around your heart. Continue wrapping the heart with the remaining ribbon until the heart is completely covered. Add a dab of glue to the end of the ribbon and press to the back side of the heart to secure.

5. You can wrap this heart again with another ribbon color or leave it as is. You can make all sorts of patterns with your ribbon or simply keep it one solid color.

Make a bunch of these hearts and hang them from doorknobs all around your house.

Beaded Heart Pipe
Cleaner Flowers

BEADED HEART PIPE CLEANER FLOWERS

These adorable beaded heart flowers will brighten a room during the Valentine's season. They are fun to bead, bend, and shape into festive heart-shaped flowers.

Learning Objectives: Children will use their fine motor skills as they manipulate the pipe cleaners; children will learn shape recognition as they make a heart; children will use hand-eye coordination as they thread the beads onto the pipe cleaners.

SUPPLIES

4 green pipe cleaners

19 large plastic pony beads per pipe cleaner (76 total), any color

Vase

STEPS

1. For each flower, thread 19 plastic beads onto one end of a pipe cleaner.
2. Hold the pipe cleaner under the bottom bead to keep all the beads at one end of the pipe cleaner. Then bend the beaded section of the pipe cleaner around and twist the top end to the bottom of the section of beads, forming a circle.
3. Bend the beaded section into a heart shape with the center pointed down.
4. Add each pipe cleaner heart flower to the vase. You can leave the vase empty or fill it with leftover pony beads.

This lovely vase of heart-shaped flowers is ready to showcase on a shelf or table for display.

MARCH

You're sure to find gold at the end of the rainbow as you create these fun March projects. Don't let that little leprechaun trick you; try to catch him and quickly grab the gold.

Glitter Clover Cards

GLITTER CLOVER CARDS

You're sure to find luck with these thumbprint clover cards. You can make them special by adding a little green or gold glitter as you create these festive cards for St. Patrick's Day.

Learning Objectives: Children will use their fine motor skills as they press ink onto their thumbs from an ink pad; children will develop art skills as they create a shamrock.

SUPPLIES

Green stamp pad

1 sheet cardstock paper, any color (per card)

White craft glue

Gold or green glitter

STEPS

1. Fold your cardstock paper into a greeting card. You can make one large card or cut your paper in half to make 2 cards per paper.

2. Firmly press your child's thumb onto the green stamp pad, then press the thumb on the middle front of the card. Do this 2 to 3 more times, close together on the card, to form the shape of a clover.

3. You can do this a few different times to create many clovers all over the card. Set the card aside to completely dry, then wash your child's thumb with soap and water.

4. Use your white craft glue to trace around the clover. You can also create a stem with your glue.

5. Place a paper towel under the card and then pour glitter on your craft glue. (The paper towel will catch any excess glitter, so you don't have a mess.) Shake the glitter around to make sure every bit of your glue is covered in glitter. Pour off any excess glitter that doesn't stick. Let the glue dry.

Give your clover card and a few gold chocolate coins to someone in need of some luck.

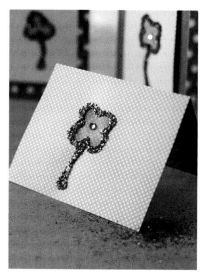

Leprechaun Gold
Coin Cookies

LEPRECHAUN GOLD COIN COOKIES

These gold coin cookies are stamped with your child's thumbprints to form a clover seal, so they look just like real leprechaun gold. Don't let any leprechauns get near the cookies or they'll take them for themselves!

Learning Objectives: Children will learn the color yellow and the shape of a circle; children will use their fine motor skills as they sprinkle sugar on the cookies.

SUPPLIES

1 roll of store-bought sugar cookie dough
Circle-shaped cookie cutter
Cookie sheet
½ cup white sugar
Yellow food coloring
Small bowl
Spoon

STEPS

1. Preheat your oven to the temperature listed on the sugar cookie directions.
2. Roll out your sugar cookie dough to ¼" thickness. Cut out lots of circles with your cookie cutter and transfer them to your cookie sheet.
3. Have your child press his or her thumb into the top of each cookie four times, creating the shape of a clover.
4. Place ½ cup of white sugar into a small bowl. Add 4–5 drops of yellow food coloring to your sugar and mix it together with a spoon. Make sure every grain of sugar is coated with the yellow coloring.
5. Sprinkle the yellow sugar on top of each cookie with a spoon, coating it well. Lightly press the sugar into the dough.
6. Bake the cookies according to the directions. Let them cool.

Eat these cookies right away, before a leprechaun comes to steal the gold.

Rainbow-Colored
Cooling Fan

RAINBOW-COLORED COOLING FAN

The weather is starting to turn warmer, so it's time to craft a paper fan. Your kids will have fun coloring the beautiful rainbow stripes on this fan, and they'll have it just in time for warm spring days.

Learning Objectives: Children will use their hand-eye coordination as they color and fold the paper; children will learn the colors of the rainbow.

SUPPLIES

1 sheet of white cardstock paper
Ruler
Crayons in the colors of a rainbow (red, orange, yellow, green, blue, and purple)
8" of red ribbon, any width

STEPS

1. With a crayon and your ruler, mark six 1½"-wide sections across your white paper. You can measure your paper either horizontally or vertically; it just depends on the finished size that you want for your paper fan.

2. Color your lined sections with each color of the rainbow, starting with a red stripe and then moving on to orange, yellow, green, blue, and ending with a purple crayon stripe.

3. After you finish coloring your paper fan, fold your paper back and forth accordion-style all the way to the end.

4. Press the bottom portion of your paper fan together with your fingers and wrap your red length of ribbon around it a few times and tie it off in a bow. This will keep the paper in a fan shape.

Spread out the top of the paper fan and begin to wave it back and forth to feel the cooling breeze of your new rainbow fan.

Rainbow Ring
Bottle Toss

RAINBOW RING BOTTLE TOSS

Save your empty glass or plastic bottles for this fun ring toss game. Try to get each of your colorful ribbon rings around the bottles for the win.

Learning Objectives: Children will work on their small motor skills and hand-eye coordination as they toss the rings around the bottle tops; children will work on fine motor skills as they wrap ribbon onto rings.

SUPPLIES

3–6 shower curtain rings

Assortment of ⅝"-wide ribbon, 2' per ring

Scissors

Craft glue or tape

6 empty glass bottles or plastic bottles filled with water or sand

STEPS

1. You can make 3–6 rings for this toss game. For each ring, wrap the end of one ribbon around one ring. Leave a 2–3" tail of ribbon so you can tie it with the other end when you finish wrapping the ribbon. Add a little bit of tape or glue to keep the ribbon in place on the ring.

2. Wrap the ribbon all the way around the ring and leave another 2–3" tail. Tie a knot with the two ends. Trim any excess ribbon strands with scissors.

3. Line up your bottles in a row or in a pyramid shape on the ground. Have your child stand 4–5' away from the bottles and try to toss each ring around a bottle. The goal is to get as many rings as possible to land on the top of each bottle.

Your child can play this ring-toss game alone or with a friend.

APRIL

Spring is in the air with the bright and cheery

projects in this chapter. Decorate for Easter,

pretend to swim sea creatures in the sea, or

create a colorful crafty umbrella for indoors.

Crushed Eggshell
Bunting

CRUSHED EGGSHELL BUNTING

Are you making lots of hard-boiled eggs this season? Make sure you keep the colored eggshells around for a fun and colorful paper bunting to hang over your front door to welcome in spring.

Learning Objectives: Children will use their fingers to crush up and sprinkle the eggshells, enhancing their fine motor skills; children will gain familiarity with letters as they spell out "spring" on the bunting; children will be exposed to different colors as they manipulate the egg shells.

SUPPLIES

Color-dyed eggshells from 12 hard-boiled eggs
White craft glue
Bowl
2 sheets of heavy white craft paper, 8½ × 11" size
Scissors
Pencil
6' of pink ribbon, ⅝"-width
Flower stickers (optional)

STEPS

1. Peel and save the shells from a dozen dyed hard-boiled eggs. You can wash these out if you like or simply let them dry completely on a paper towel overnight.

2. After the eggshells are completely dry, crush and crunch them up into tiny shell bits and place them into a bowl.

3. With your scissors, cut out 6 large, isosceles triangles from the craft paper for the bunting, using the photo as a guide. You can get 3 triangles out of one 8½ × 11" paper.

4. Place the triangles upside down in a row. Use a pencil to spell out "SPRING," in capital letters, on the triangles, with one letter on each triangle.

5. Trace each letter on the triangles with your craft glue. Sprinkle your crushed eggshells onto the glue. Carefully shake off any excess eggshells back into the bowl. Let these letters dry completely.

6. Once the glue is dry, line up your triangles corner to corner. Place your ribbon across the top of each triangle and glue it in place, making sure to leave enough hanging off each end of "SPRING" so you can hang the bunting. Let your banner dry completely.

You can add a few flower stickers on the ribbon for decoration. Now your spring eggshell banner is ready to hang up and brighten your home for spring.

Chocolate-Dipped
Crispy Rice Eggs

CHOCOLATE-DIPPED CRISPY RICE EGGS

Have fun celebrating Easter as you create and dip these egg-shaped cereal treats. The Easter Bunny is sure to hide these eggs in a special spot. They are the perfect dessert after an Easter meal and are a great way for your kids to help you in the kitchen.

Learning Objectives: Children will learn shape recognition as they form an oval shape for this treat; children will use cooking skills as they work with the cereal and dip the egg shapes in white chocolate.

SUPPLIES

5 cups crispy rice cereal

4 cups miniature marshmallows

½ cup butter

Large saucepan

Cooking spray

Microwave-safe bowl

Wax paper

12 oz. bag of white chocolate chips

Bowl and 2 spoons for dipping

Homemade or store-bought colored frosting for decorating (optional)

STEPS

1. In a large saucepan over medium heat, melt the butter and marshmallows. Once this mix is melted, remove the pan from the heat and add your cereal. Stir your mix and pour it onto wax paper to cool slightly.

2. Once the cereal mix has cooled slightly, grease your hands lightly with cooking spray and grab a handful of the mix and shape it into an oval egg shape and set aside. Continue making egg shapes until you use up all of the cereal mix.

3. Melt the white chocolate in the microwave for 1 minute in a microwave-safe bowl. Take it out and stir. If it needs more time, microwave the chocolate again at 15-second intervals until it is completely melted.

4. Place one oval-shaped treat onto a spoon and dip it into the chocolate. Use a second spoon to help cover the entire treat in chocolate. Set the treat back on the wax paper to harden. Dip each of your remaining egg-shaped treats in chocolate and set aside to dry.

5. Once the chocolate egg treats are cool and hard, you can leave them as is or decorate them with colorful frosting.

Place your crispy egg treats in a festive basket, ready for snacking during the Easter season.

Watercolor Coffee
Filter Umbrella

WATERCOLOR COFFEE FILTER UMBRELLA

April showers are here and will bring flowers in May. Pretend to stay dry with your own miniature watercolor coffee filter umbrella.

Learning Objectives: Children will use their creativity as they use watercolors to paint their paper umbrella; children will use their imagination as they pretend play with their paper umbrella.

SUPPLIES

1 coffee filter (per umbrella)

Watercolor paints

Paintbrush

1 cup water

2 pipe cleaners, any color (per umbrella)

Hole punch

STEPS

1. Paint your coffee filter with your watercolors and paintbrush. Use your cup of water to wash out your brush as you change paint colors. Add all sorts of colors and shapes to your coffee filter. Let this dry completely.

2. Twist your 2 pipe cleaners together.

3. Use your hole punch to make 2 small holes about ¼" apart in the center of your painted coffee filter (see photo). Thread your twisted pipe cleaner through the 2 holes and twist the end onto the longer piece to hold the pipe cleaner in place.

4. Bend the bottom end of your pipe cleaner in a letter J shape to form the bottom of an umbrella.

Start singing in the rain with your new watercolor umbrella.

Egg Carton
Sea Creatures

EGG CARTON SEA CREATURES

Swim and soar all around with these egg-carton sea creatures. You can make all kinds of sea animals by recycling egg cartons and turning them into creatures from the sea.

Learning Objectives: Children will have fun with creativity as they design and color a variety of sea creatures; children will use their imagination as they pretend play with their creatures; children will gain animal recognition as they create each sea animal.

SUPPLIES

1 dozen-egg carton

Scissors

Craft glue

Red, green, blue, orange, and yellow craft paint

Paintbrush

1 sheet red craft paper

2 red pipe cleaners

1 green pipe cleaner

12 googly eyes

2–3' of red ribbon, ¼" width

Black crayons

STEPS

1. With your scissors, cut the lid off your egg carton. Cut out 8 individual sections and leave 1 group of 4 sections in a row; adult cutting preferred.

2. Use these egg cartons to create the following sea creatures with paint, glue, and craft paper.

   Crab: Paint a single egg-carton piece red and let it dry. With a pencil, punch 2 small holes on one side, just below the round part of the egg carton, using the photo as a guide. Thread two 1" pieces of red pipe cleaner into the holes and bend them up to secure them. Glue 1 googly eye to the top of each pipe cleaner for the crab's eyes. For the pincers, cut out two 4 × ½" strips of red craft paper and glue them on the inside of the egg carton, under the crab. You can also use a black crayon to draw a smile onto the crab's face.

   Octopus: Paint a single egg-carton piece with any color and let it dry. Cut out 8 strips of red ribbon, about 3–4" long each. Glue the ribbon strips onto the inside of the egg carton piece (so they dangle when you turn over the egg-carton piece). Glue 2 googly eyes onto the front, using the photo as guide. This creature could also represent a jellyfish.

   Clam: You will need 2 egg-carton pieces. Paint these any color you like and let them dry. Using the photo as a guide, hold the cut edges of the 2 pieces together and glue one side of both pieces to each other so it looks like a clam chomping down. Glue on 2 googly eyes.

   Fish: You will need 3 egg-carton pieces. Glue around the entire top edge of 2 egg-carton pieces and press them together. Let them dry. Glue the third egg-carton piece to the bottom of the glued piece, but facing in the opposite direction. Use the photo as a guide. Paint this fish any color you like and let it dry. Glue 2 googly eyes on the fish, one on each side of its head.

   Sea snake: You will need the 4-section egg-carton piece. Paint this piece any color you like and let it dry. Glue 2 googly eyes onto the side of one end piece for the head. Twist a 3" piece of red pipe cleaner to form a tongue for the snake. Then glue the tongue to the inside of the creature's head.

   Sea turtle: You will need a single egg-carton piece. Paint this piece green and let it dry. With yellow paint, draw lines to form the segments of a turtle's shell. For the turtle's head, form a 3" piece of green pipe cleaner into a lollipop shape (a circle on top with a long double line to represent the stick) and twist the ends together at the bottom. Glue the straight end to the inside of the carton piece. Glue 2 googly eyes to the top of the circle head.

Pretend to swim your sea creatures around the house or over a blue-colored blanket that represents the ocean.

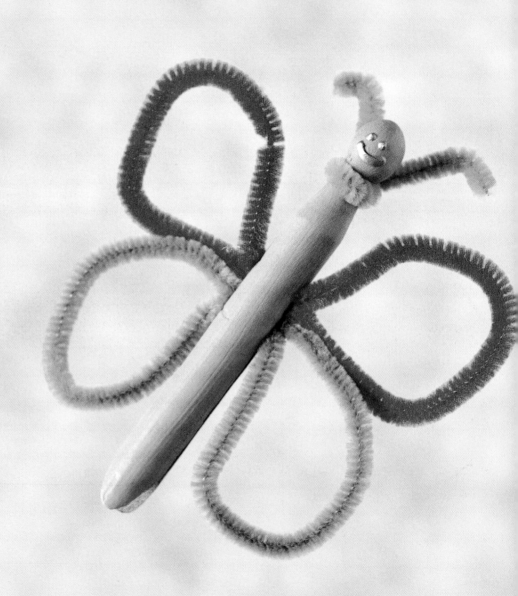

MAY

Whether you're celebrating Cinco de Mayo,

Mother's Day, or even just the season of spring,

you'll find all kinds of fun projects for May in

this chapter, including flowers, cards, butterflies,

and sombreros.

Tissue Paper Flower
Mother's Day Card

TISSUE PAPER FLOWER MOTHER'S DAY CARD

This Mother's Day, show your Mom how much you love her by creating this darling tissue paper flower card. You can create a bright pom-pom flower to make your card really pop.

Learning Objectives: Children will use their artistic skills as they make a flower with tissue paper; children will use their fine motor skills as they twist and bunch the flower.

SUPPLIES

1 sheet 8½ × 11" cardstock paper, any color

1 sheet 1½ × 3" cardstock paper, any color

2 sheets tissue paper, any color

1 green pipe cleaner

1 sheet green letter stickers

Scissors

Green crayon

Craft glue

STEPS

1. Fold the largest piece of cardstock paper in half to make a card.
2. Cut a 1" piece of green pipe cleaner and set it aside.
3. Cut six 3"-diameter circles out of your tissue paper. Lay the circles on top of each other. With your fingers, bunch all the flowers together and pinch them together in the center.
4. Twist the green pipe cleaner piece around the center of the tissue paper to secure it. Fluff out the tissue paper to make a paper pom-pom flower, as shown in the photo.
5. Glue your pom-pom flower onto the left side of the front of your card. With your crayon, draw a green stem from the bottom of the flower to the bottom of the card. You can draw leaves on the stem, too.
6. On the right side of the card, glue the small piece of cardstock paper vertically on the card so it is next to the flower. With your green letter stickers, add the word "MOM" on top of the small vertical paper.

Write a few things you love about your Mom on the inside of the card and then the card is ready for Mother's Day.

Cinco de Mayo
Sombrero Cupcakes

CINCO DE MAYO SOMBRERO CUPCAKES

Children can celebrate Cinco de Mayo with these miniature sombrero cupcakes. After one bite, they'll want to say, "Olé."

Learning Objectives: Children will use cooking skills as they help you bake in the kitchen; children will use their imagination as they create miniature edible sombreros.

SUPPLIES

- 1 package pre-made sugar cookie dough
- ¼ cup red and green sprinkles, mixed together
- Baking sheet
- 1 container store-bought white frosting
- 12 large white gumdrops
- 12 white pre-baked cupcakes

STEPS

1. Preheat the oven to the temperature listed on the sugar cookie directions.
2. Form 12 balls from the sugar cookie dough. Roll each of the balls into the red-and-green sprinkle mixture, making sure to cover every area of the dough ball.
3. Place each sprinkled dough ball on a baking sheet and bake your cookies according to the recipe's directions. Let these cookies cool.
4. Add a drop of white frosting to the bottom of a large white gumdrop and place the gumdrop onto the center of the baked sugar cookie. Add a little bit of white frosting around the bottom edge of the gumdrop to secure it in place. Add more red-and-green sprinkles to the cookie to cover the white frosting. This cookie represents a sombrero. Repeat this step with all remaining cookies and gumdrops.
5. Frost your 12 pre-baked cupcakes with white frosting. Place 1 gumdrop sugar cookie on the top of each cupcake.

These festive cupcakes are ready to serve for a Cinco de Mayo celebration.

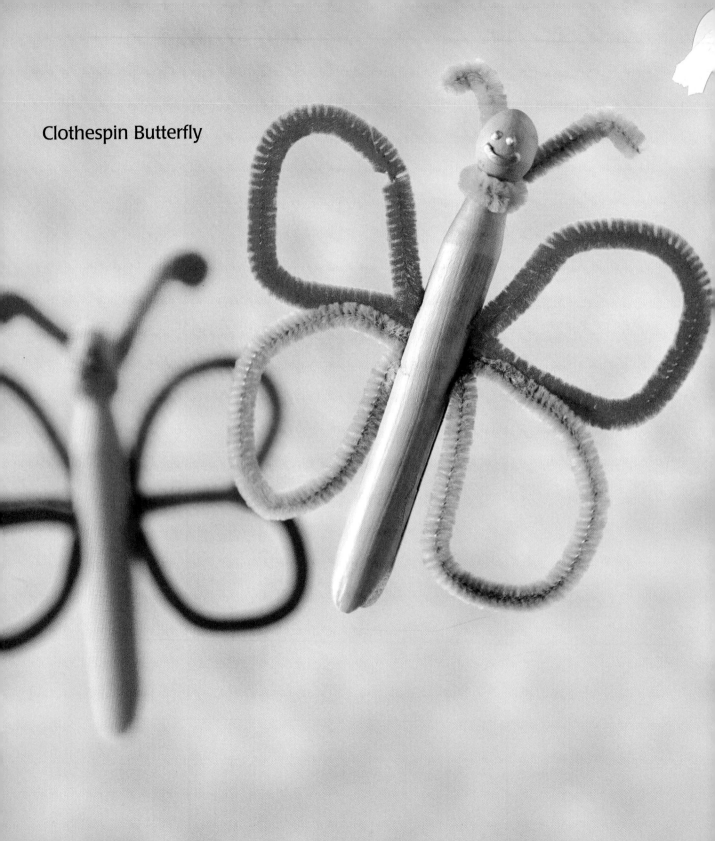

Clothespin Butterfly

CLOTHESPIN BUTTERFLY

These butterflies are all aflutter as they float and fly around. Buzz them by a few flowers as you pretend they are ready to drink some nectar.

Learning Objectives: Children will use their imagination as they create a toy butterfly; children will act out their imagination with pretend play; children will gain a sense of science skills as they create a butterfly.

SUPPLIES

Peg-style wooden clothespin
(1 per butterfly)
Craft paint, any color
Paintbrush
2 pipe cleaners, any color
(per butterfly)
1 black pipe cleaner

STEPS

1. Using your paintbrush and paint, color your clothespin any color you like. Decorate it with lines or swirls or polka dots if you want. You can even add a tiny little face at the top of the clothespin, complete with eyes and a smile. Set your clothespin aside to dry.

2. Using the diagram as a guide, take 1 colored pipe cleaner and fold each end back to the center to form 2 elongated circles and twist them together. This will make the top set of wings. Do this again with another pipe cleaner, forming the bottom set of butterfly wings.

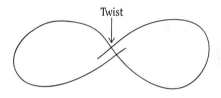

3. When your clothespin is dry, slip the center of each pipe cleaner wing through the opening of the clothespin. Using the photo as a guide, slide each wing up to the top of the opening.

4. Cut the black pipe cleaner in half. Twist it around the neck of the clothespin butterfly, leaving the 2 ends of the pipe cleaner sticking out and up, to represent the butterfly's antennae. You can also bend down the tops ¼" to give them more dimension.

Now your butterfly is ready to fly through the air, catch the wind, and look for fun.

Foam Flower Crowns

FOAM FLOWER CROWNS

Your children can fly around like fairies with these foam flower crowns. They are the perfect craft for the season as they help welcome in springtime.

Learning Objectives: Children will use their fine motor skills as they cut out and lace each flower with elastic; children will enjoy pretend play as they dance around in their flower crowns.

SUPPLIES

2–3 craft foam sheets, any color

Scissors

Hole punch

10–12" of ¼"-wide elastic per headband

Stapler or sewing machine with white thread

Pencil

STEPS

1. Using the photo as a guide, draw a 1–2"-wide 6-petal flower from the craft foam with your pencil. Use this flower as a template and draw 11 or 12 more flowers onto the craft foam. You can use all the same color of craft foam or incorporate 2–3 different colors for the flowers.
2. With your scissors, cut out each flower from your craft foam sheets.
3. Punch 2 holes into the center of each flower with your hole punch. Make sure the holes are about ½" apart.
4. Measure the elastic around your child's head to make sure it is the right length. The elastic needs to fit snugly around your child's head, but overlap it by about 1". Trim off the excess elastic.
5. Thread the elastic through each hole of each flower. Lace all of the flowers onto the elastic. You can create a color pattern as you lace the flowers or you can simply lace the flowers randomly.
6. After all of your flowers are laced onto the elastic, staple the two ends together. Or you can sew the two ends of elastic together with a sewing machine or a needle and thread.

Dance around and play with your new flower crowns for spring.

JUNE

It's summer and time to have some fun. Create a gift for Father's Day or get creative for a fun day out in the sun.

Tissue Box Remote
Control Holder

TISSUE BOX REMOTE CONTROL HOLDER

In your family, who is always looking for the remote control? Dad. This is the perfect project to help your Dad keep track of his remote. And it makes a perfect Father's Day gift.

Learning Objectives: Children will learn about giving gifts as they create this craft for someone else; children will use their creativity as they craft and paint this project.

SUPPLIES

2 empty square-shaped tissue boxes

Scissors

1 sheet of black letter stickers

Decoupage glue and sealer

Sponge brush

6 sheets of 4¼ × 5" craft paper, any color

Craft glue

STEPS

1. Cut off the top of 1 of the tissue boxes and set the box aside.

2. Tear open the second box on both sides, as shown in the first diagram. Cut off the top and bottom sections of the box, which will leave you with 4 pieces, as shown in the second diagram. Discard the top and bottom sections, leaving the 2 remaining sides.

3. With the 2 remaining side pieces, glue together the flaps of each side to form a new *rectangular*-shaped box. Use the last two diagrams as a guide. This rectangular box is the middle piece of the remote control holder and fits inside the first square-shaped box.

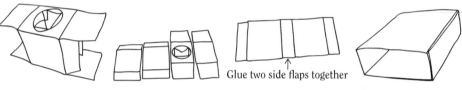
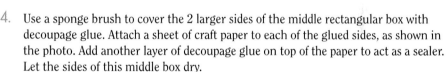

Glue two side flaps together

4. Use a sponge brush to cover the 2 larger sides of the middle rectangular box with decoupage glue. Attach a sheet of craft paper to each of the glued sides, as shown in the photo. Add another layer of decoupage glue on top of the paper to act as a sealer. Let the sides of this middle box dry.

5. Use your craft glue to glue the middle piece into the center of the first tissue box. Let this dry completely.

6. With your black letter stickers, spell out "Where's the Remote?" on one of the remaining 4¼ × 5" pieces of craft paper.

7. Cover all 4 sides of the outside of the *square* box with decoupage glue. Attach the lettered craft paper to 1 side of the square box, as shown in the photo. Then attach the last 3 pieces of 4¼ × 5" craft paper to cover the remaining sides of the square box. Press each paper on and let them dry for a few minutes.

8. Add another layer of decoupage glue to the outside of each paper attached to the box to give it a finished and sealed look. Let this dry completely.

Now this box is ready to hold your family's remote controls and keep them in one handy place.

Father's Day
Meatball Golf Clubs

FATHER'S DAY MEATBALL GOLF CLUBS

Make a Father's Day meal a little more memorable by having your kids help you cook dinner for Dad. He'll want to make a hole-in-one with these edible golf clubs made from meatballs and breadsticks.

Learning Objectives: Children will use fine motor skills as they make these meatball golf clubs; children will use their imagination because the meatballs represent golf clubs.

SUPPLIES

- 1 lb. bag of store-bought pre-cooked meatballs, 1–2" size
- 1 box of thin hard breadsticks
- ¼ cup miniature marshmallows (optional)
- 1 cup BBQ sauce (optional)

STEPS

1. Warm up your meatballs according to the package directions and let them sit until they are cool enough to touch.
2. Break each of your breadsticks in half. Press one half into the center of a pre-cooked meatball to make it look like a golf club.
3. Continue to press breadsticks into the meatballs until you have 20 meatball golf clubs on a plate.
4. For display, add a white miniature marshmallow next to each meatball golf club to represent the golf ball.

Add a bowl of BBQ sauce for dinner and your golf clubs are ready to dip and eat!

Milk Jug Toss Game

MILK JUG TOSS GAME

Catch beanbags, sponges, or rolled-up socks in these catchers recycled from milk jugs. Make it a game and see how far away you can stand as you try to catch beanbags in these milk jug catchers.

Learning Objectives: Children will learn cooperation as they play this game with a friend; children will learn hand-eye coordination as they try to catch a beanbag in the hole of the catcher; children will use muscle control as they throw their beanbag and lift their catcher.

SUPPLIES

1 recycled gallon-size milk jug
(per person)

Scissors (adult only)

Stickers, any shape or color

Ribbons, any color, various
lengths and widths

2–3 beanbags, sponges, or
rolled-up socks

STEPS

1. Rinse out your milk jug and allow it to air-dry.
2. With your scissors (adult only), cut an opening along the top of the milk jug and continue cutting around in a half circle, as shown in the diagram.

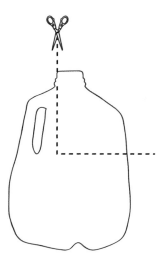

3. Decorate your milk jug with stickers.
4. Cut six pieces of colored ribbon about 6" long each. Wrap a piece of ribbon around the handle of the milk jug and tie the two ends together in a knot, letting the ends hang loose. Repeat with the remaining ribbon until the entire handle is covered with ribbons, as shown in the photo.

Play a toss game with a friend. Stand about 5' away from your friend and toss a beanbag into the air and have your friend catch it with the milk jug catcher. Then your friend can toss the beanbag back and you can try to catch it in your milk jug catcher.

Paper Tube Rattlesnake

PAPER TUBE RATTLESNAKE

This rattlesnake is just itching to be created with a few empty paper-towel tubes. I'm sure you've got a few lying around after the paper towels are all used. Instead of sending them to the recycle bin, craft them into a silly, slithering snake.

Learning Objectives: Children will use art skills as they paint and color; children will pretend play as they manipulate their snake; children will gain a sense of biology as they create a snake; children will use fine motor skills as they thread yarn through the snake tubes.

SUPPLIES

3 paper-towel tubes or
    1 wrapping-paper tube
Scissors
2–3' of red yarn
Craft paint, any color
Paintbrushes
Newspaper
Hole punch
5–6 large plastic pony beads
2 googly eyes
Craft glue or glue dots

STEPS

1. Start by painting your paper tubes. You can paint them all one color, such as green, or divide your tubes into 2 or 3 groups and paint them different colors. After painting, set the tubes on a piece of newspaper to air-dry.

2. Once the tubes are dry, you can paint on some snake-like designs. For example, the snake in the photos has yellow and orange spots. Let these dry once again on the newspaper.

3. Use your scissors to cut the paper tubes into 1–2" pieces. The tubes may bend in half as you're cutting, but you can easily bend them back into shape.

4. With one of the paper tube pieces, punch a hole with your hole punch and securely tie one end of your yarn to it, leaving 4–5" of yarn at the end to use as the tail. Then thread the long end of the yarn through the remaining paper tube pieces to form your snake.

5. When you finish threading the last tube, punch a hole in the first tube piece, leaving 4–5" of yarn at the end. Tie the yarn to the hole, but leave the tail hanging out to act as the snake's tongue.

6. On the tail end of the yarn, add 5–6 pony beads. Tie off the yarn at the end to hold the beads in place. This will act as the snake's rattle.

7. Glue 2 googly eyes to the top of the snake's head.

Now this rattlesnake is ready for some slithering. Start practicing your hisssssssssing sounds!

JULY

Celebrate your country's Independence Day by making a few of these crafts in July. Or simply keep summer alive with an ice cream treat and a game of tic-tac-toe.

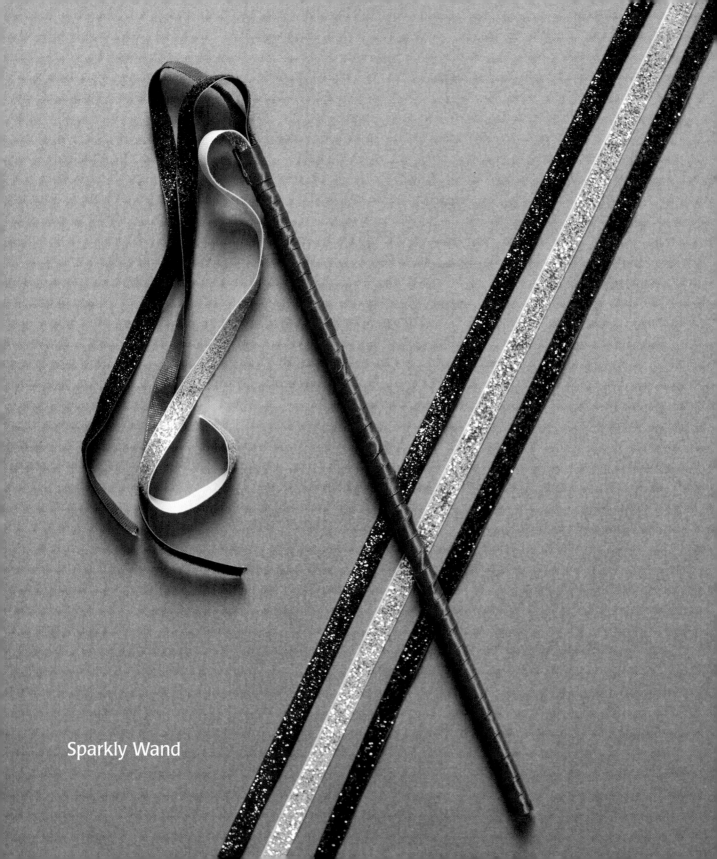

Sparkly Wand

SPARKLY WAND

This super-sparkly wand is fun to make for any occasion. You can create this red-white-and-blue wand to help keep the fireworks sparkling on the Fourth of July.

Learning Objectives: Children will develop their gross motor skills as they move around and dance with their wands; children will work on hand-eye coordination as they wrap ribbon around a wooden dowel.

SUPPLIES

12" wooden dowel, ¼" diameter
3' of red ribbon, any width
8" of red sparkly ribbon
8" of silver sparkly ribbon
8" of blue sparkly ribbon
Craft glue

STEPS

1. On one end of your wooden dowel, add 3 small dabs of glue. Attach each of your 8" strips of sparkly ribbon to the glue end of the dowel, as shown in the photo. Hold these in place until they are dry.

2. Add a dab of glue to the other end of your wooden dowel. Attach one end of your 3' of red ribbon to the glue and start to wrap your ribbon around the dowel.

3. Wrap your ribbon around and around the dowel until it reaches the other end. Cut your ribbon at this end and add another dab of glue to secure it in place. Let the glue dry.

This wand is ready to use as sparkler as you celebrate the Fourth of July.

Red and Blue Berry
Ice Cream Boat

RED AND BLUE BERRY ICE CREAM BOAT

Sail this ice cream boat right onto your dessert table. You won't be able to resist the red and blue berries sitting on top of your vanilla ice cream.

Learning Objectives: Children will learn the colors red, white, and blue; children will learn the shape of a star.

SUPPLIES

3-4 scoops of vanilla ice cream
Small bowl and spoon
¼ cup strawberries
¼ cup raspberries
¼ cup blueberries
1 lollipop stick or toothpick
1 small piece of yellow craft paper
Scissors
Tape or craft glue

STEPS

1. Add 3–4 scoops of vanilla ice cream to a small bowl.
2. Pour your strawberries, raspberries, and blueberries on top of the ice cream.
3. Cut a small yellow star out of your craft paper. Use craft glue or tape to attach it to the top of a lollipop stick or a toothpick. Place your star stick in the center of your bowl through the ice cream.

Add a spoon and you've got smooth sailing right into your mouth. I'm sure you and your kids will see fireworks while eating this yummy holiday treat.

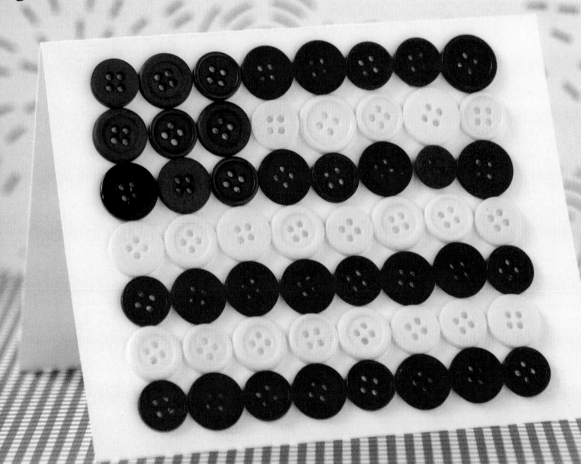

Flag Button Card

FLAG BUTTON CARD

Button up this darling American flag card. It's the perfect way to show your patriotic spirit to celebrate the Fourth of July. Or, for a different take, you can teach your child about another country by using buttons in colors that represent another country's flag.

Learning Objectives: Children will use fine motor skills as they manipulate the buttons; children will recognize colors as they recreate their country's flag.

SUPPLIES

26 red buttons, ³/₈" or ¹/₂" size
21 white buttons, ³/₈" or ¹/₂" size
9 blue buttons, ³/₈" or ¹/₂" size
Craft glue
1 sheet heavy white cardstock
   paper, 8¹/₂ × 11" size
Scissors

STEPS

1. Cut your paper in half to make two 5½ × 8½" pieces. This will give you 2 pieces to make 2 cards. Fold 1 piece in half to form your card.

2. Using the photo as a guide, place your buttons on the front side of your card into the shape of the American flag: 9 blue buttons on the top left corner, and alternating rows of red and white buttons to form the stripes. This card has 7 rows with 8 columns of buttons.

3. To glue on the buttons, you can either mark each button's place with a pencil through the hole of the button, or you can simply start gluing on the first few buttons and eyeball the placement of the rest as you go.

4. Continue to glue each button in place on the front of the card until you have created your flag. Let these buttons dry completely.

Now your card is ready for display as you honor your country's flag.

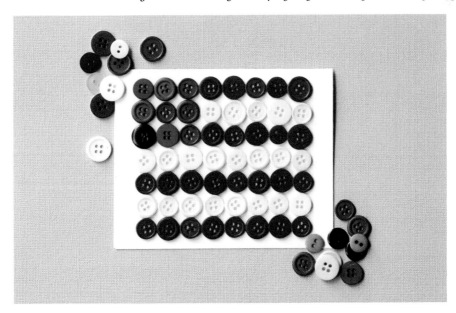

Tissue Box Tic-Tac-Toe

TISSUE BOX TIC-TAC-TOE

Play a game of tic-tac-toe by tossing beanbags or rolled-up socks into these recycled tissue boxes.

Learning Objectives: Children will learn hand-eye coordination as they toss beanbags into each box, as well as when they manipulate a paintbrush; children will learn cooperation as they learn to take turns while playing the game of tic-tac-toe.

SUPPLIES

9 empty cube-shaped tissue boxes

Scissors

Craft paint, any color

Paintbrushes

Hot glue (adult only) or craft glue

10 beanbags (or rolled-up socks) in 2 colors, 5 of one and 5 of another

STEPS

1. For each tissue box, cut the top off with scissors, leaving an opening at the top.
2. Using your glue, attach the 9 tissue boxes together to form a 3 × 3 grid of boxes, as shown in the photo. Once formed, let it dry completely.
3. Paint the outside of your newly formed 3 × 3 boxed grid with any color of paint and a paintbrush. Try to get paint onto every area of the box. You can paint the top of the grid as well, covering the tops of the boxes as much as possible above where it is glued. You don't need to paint the bottom of the boxed grid. Let the paint dry completely.

Now gather your beanbags or socks and find a friend to play the game of tic-tac-toe using your tissue box game board.

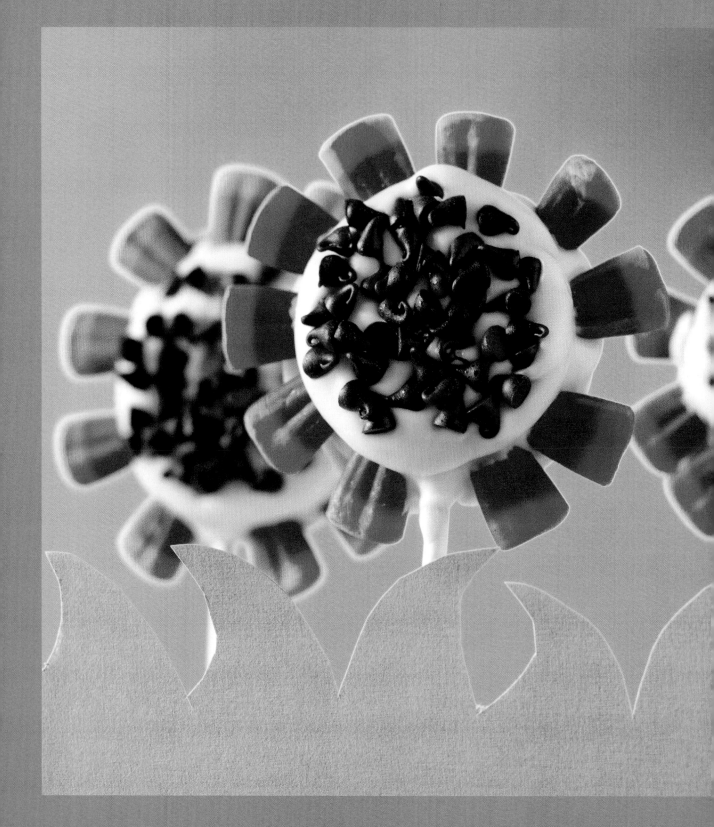

AUGUST

Your summer will still be going strong as your family sits by your crafty campfire, floats your bubble rafts, and snacks on tasty sunflower cookies. Even the birds might want to stop by to feast on your pine cone garland.

Pine Cone Bird
Feeder Garland

PINE CONE BIRD FEEDER GARLAND

Hang this bird feeder garland in your yard to help feed your feathered friends. Enjoy watching birds drop by for a snack that you provided.

Learning Objectives: Children will learn responsibility as they care for and feed backyard birds; children will use their fine motor skills as they roll their pine cones in peanut butter and birdseed.

SUPPLIES

10' of ribbon, any color and width

Scissors

4 large pine cones

½ cup peanut butter

½ cup birdseed

2 plates

STEPS

1. Spread ½ cup of peanut butter onto one plate and ½ cup of birdseed onto a second plate.
2. Take a pine cone and roll it in the peanut butter and then roll it in the birdseed. Repeat this process with the rest of the pine cones.
3. Cut your ribbon into 2 different lengths: one 4' piece and four 18" pieces.
4. Tie an 18" piece of ribbon around the top of each of the 4 pine cones.
5. Tie each of the 4 ribbons with pinecones onto the longest length of ribbon. Space them about a foot apart, leaving 6" of ribbon hanging loosely from each end.
6. Attach your pine-cone garland to a fence in your yard by tying each end to a fence post. If your garland is heavy and droops too much in the center, then you can use a little more ribbon to attach the center of the garland to the fence as well.

Your pine cone bird feeder garland is now ready for your feathered friends to snack on.

Sunflower Cookie
Lollipops

SUNFLOWER COOKIE LOLLIPOPS

Give a little sunshine to someone in your life with these cookies on a stick. Dip and decorate them into fun sunflower cookie lollipops.

Learning Objectives: Children will learn to recognize the shape of a flower; children will use fine motor skills as they place candies onto these flowers; children will use their imagination as they create a flower cookie.

SUPPLIES

4 cream-filled sandwich cookies
4 lollipop sticks
1 bag of white chocolate chips
Wax paper
Microwave-safe bowl
1 bag of candy corn (10 pieces per lollipop)
1 bag of miniature chocolate chips

STEPS

1. Insert a lollipop stick into the center of each of your cream-filled cookies. If you need to, open the cookie, place on the stick, and close the cookie together again. Lay each lollipop on a flat tray.

2. Place your white chocolate chips in a bowl and melt in the microwave for 1 minute. Take out and stir. If the chocolate is not quite melted, place the bowl back into the microwave for 15 second intervals until the chocolate is melted smooth.

3. Carefully dip a cookie lollipop into the melted white chocolate until it is completely covered. Lay the lollipop onto a piece of wax paper. Do this for each of the remaining cookies.

4. Before the white chocolate hardens, add 20–30 mini chocolate chips on top of the cookie to represent the sunflower seeds. You want to cover the entire front side of the cookie. Gently press down so the chips stay in place.

5. While the white chocolate is still wet, add your candy corn all around the cookies to represent the flower petals. Place the candy corn point-side-down all around the sides of each cookie and into the cream centers.

6. Let the cookies harden. It might take a few hours for them to harden or you can speed up the process by placing the cookies into the freezer or refrigerator.

Once the chocolate on the cookies is hard, carefully peel the cookies off the wax paper and enjoy them as a fun sunshine snack.

Bubble Wrap Raft

BUBBLE WRAP RAFT

Reuse your leftover bubble wrap by turning it into a fun water raft. Lazily float this raft in the bathtub or sink, or even down a kid-friendly river carrying all sorts of cargo.

Learning Objectives: Children will observe science as they float their raft; children will learn balance as they help their raft float.

SUPPLIES

4 × 5" piece of bubble wrap
1 plastic drinking straw
1 sheet craft foam, any color
Hot glue (adult use only)
Scissors
1 pipe cleaner, any color (for optional figurine)

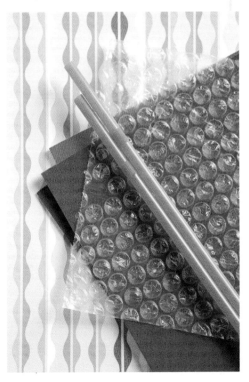

STEPS

1. Cut your craft foam into a 2 × 2" triangle. Cut a small ¼" slit at the top and at the bottom of the triangle, as shown on the diagram.

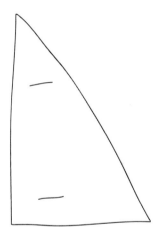

2. With your scissors, cut your drinking straw so you have a 5" piece. Slip this straw piece into the slits of the foam triangle. This is the raft's sail.

3. Put a large drop of glue on the center top of the bubble wrap, about 2" away from the edge. Place your straw into the glue and hold it in place until the glue dries. The glue should only take a few minutes to harden.

4. Once the glue is dry, fill up your sink or outdoor pool with water and place your bubble wrap raft onto the water.

Your raft should float on top of the water. Have your child place a favorite toy on the raft so it can go for a ride. Or have your child make a figurine from a pipe cleaner and place it on the raft.

Flameless Kid's
Campfire

FLAMELESS KID'S CAMPFIRE

Kids can build a playtime flameless campfire that is great for indoor or outdoor use. Cozy up to the flameless fire and tell all kinds of campfire stories beside the glowing light.

Learning Objectives: Children will use science skills as they learn about a campfire; children will use their fine motor skills as they build the flameless fire; children will use construction techniques as they build this flameless campfire.

SUPPLIES

2 empty paper towel tubes
Scissors
Craft glue
1 large sheet red tissue paper
1 large sheet yellow tissue paper
1 large sheet orange tissue paper
2–3 glow sticks

STEPS

1. Cut each paper towel tube in half. Lay 2 tube pieces together in one direction. Stack the other 2 tubes on top but facing the other direction so the tube sets are perpendicular to one another. (Use the photo as a guide.) Glue the tubes in place to create the pretend firewood.

2. Lay the 3 sheets of tissue paper on top of each other. Gather all three together at the center, creating a sort of stem at the center with the tissue paper. Add glue to the bottom stem of the gathered tissue paper and set the end into the center of the paper towel firewood structure. This will create the illusion of fire.

3. Crack your glow sticks and place them inside the tissue paper by simply dropping them in the center of the tissue paper "flame."

Now turn off the lights and your family can enjoy sitting by a warm and cozy fire.

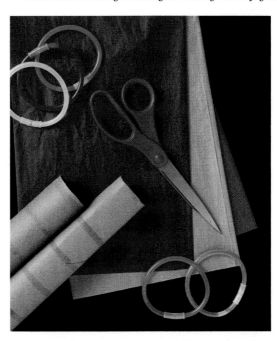

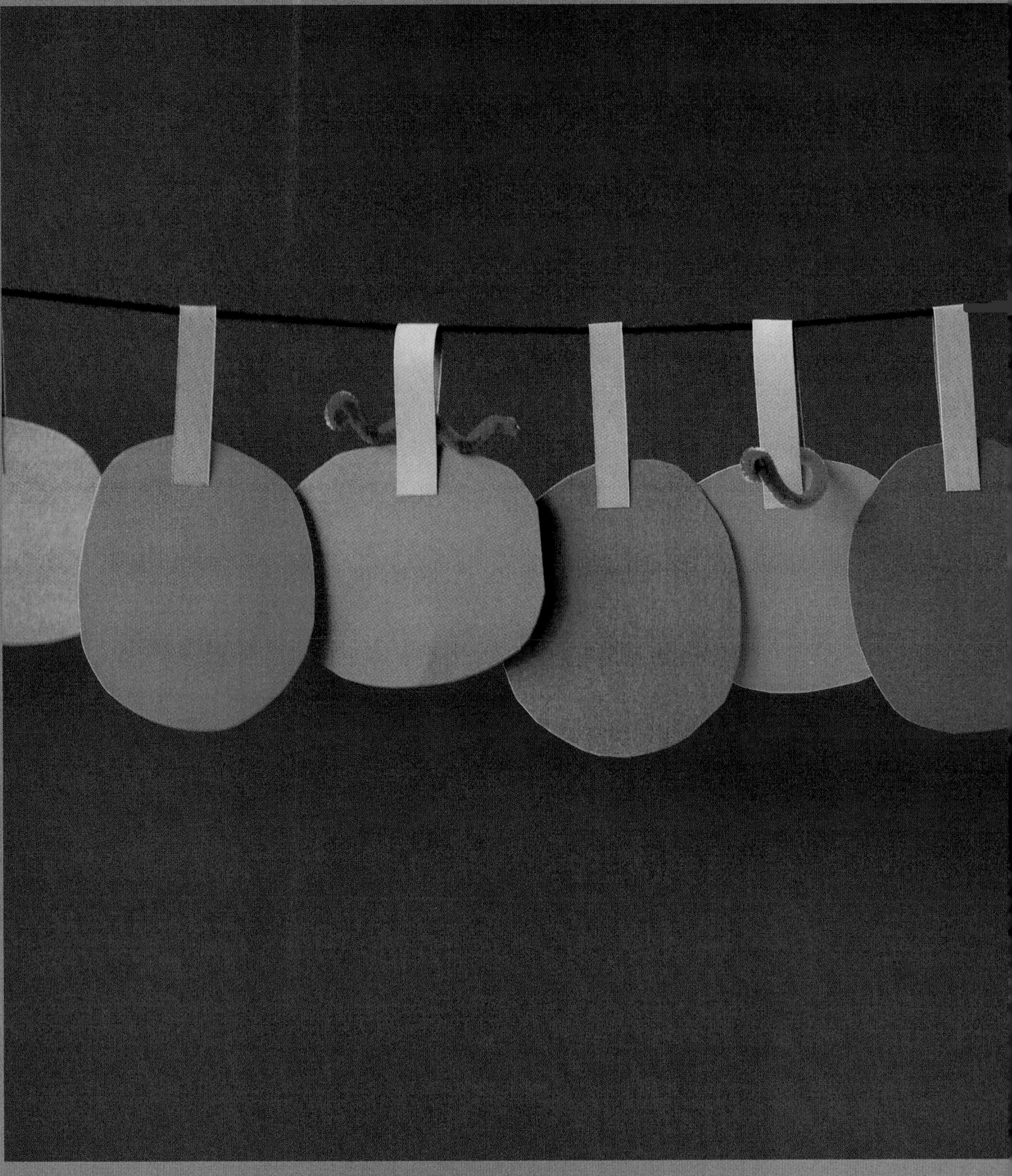

SEPTEMBER

Fall is the perfect time for crafting. The
weather is cooling down and school is back in
session. Your child can give a fun apple picture
or a pet rock to a teacher.

Teacher's Pet Rock Paperweight

A+
Name Sarah
1. cat
2. hat
3. sat
4. fat
5. mat
6. pat
7. vat
8. bat

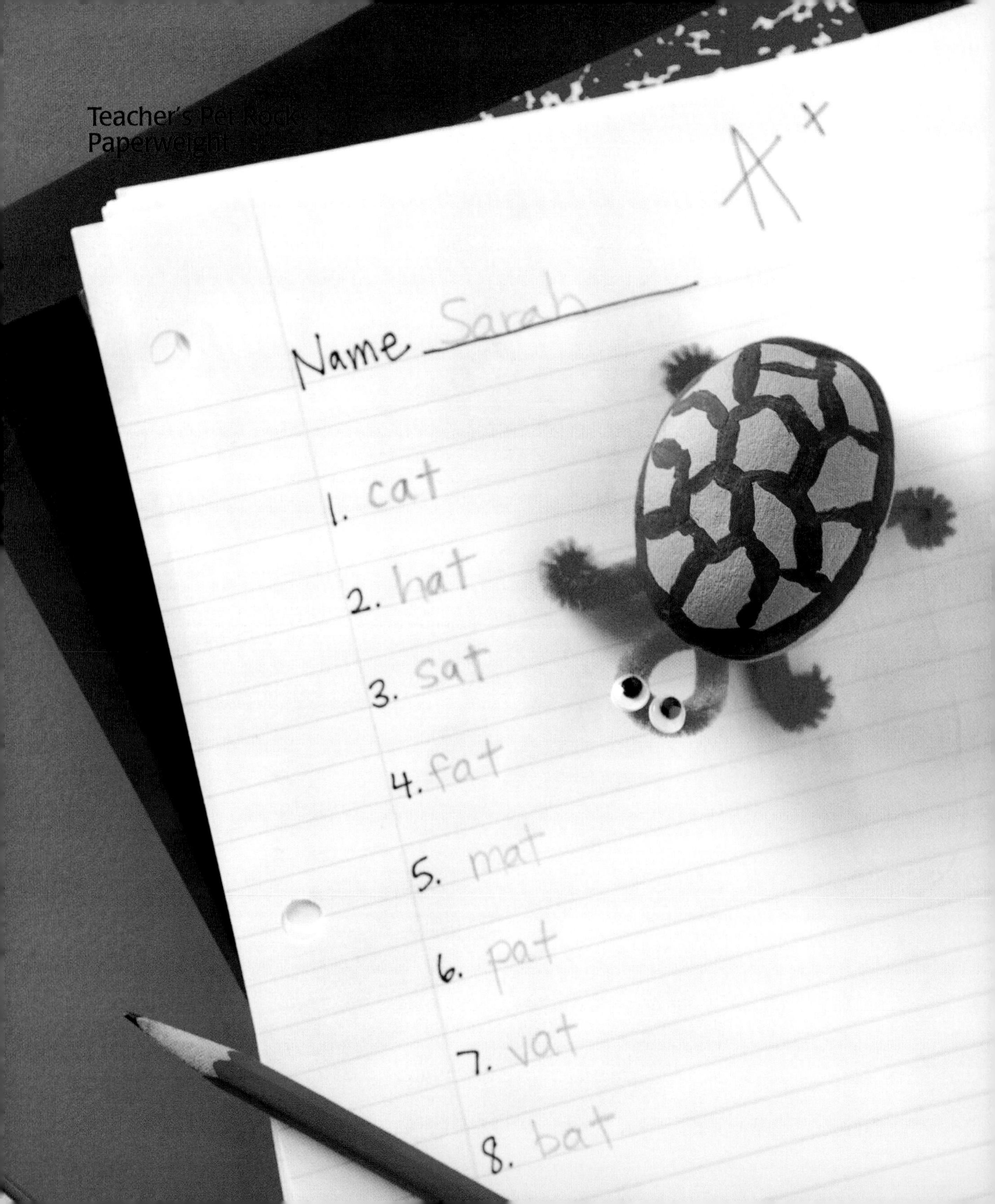

TEACHER'S PET ROCK PAPERWEIGHT

Dress up a friendly little rock into a paperweight pet. Any school teacher would love to receive this craft as a gift from an admiring student.

Learning Objectives: Children will learn to share as they create and give this rock to a beloved teacher; children will use hand-eye coordination as they manipulate a paintbrush; children will experience science as they work with a heavy solid rock, seeing how it can become a paperweight.

SUPPLIES

1 smooth rock, 2-3" width

Craft paint, any color

Paintbrush

Hot glue (adult only) or craft glue

2 googly eyes

Newspaper

Craft fur or feathers (optional)

Pipe cleaner assortment (optional)

Pom-poms (optional)

STEPS

1. Wash and dry your rock.
2. Using paints and a paintbrush, color your rock any color. Give it layers of color, with stripes, dots, or swirls. Set the rock aside on a newspaper to dry.
3. Glue 2 googly eyes to the front of the rock. Glue on craft feathers, fur, or even pom-poms, whatever your child would like to add to create his or her pet rock.
4. Add any other embellishments that would make this a cute little pet. You can make it a bunny, turtle, bird, dog, cat, spider, and so on.

Once the glue and paint on your rock are dry, it's ready to give away as a gift. Your child's teacher can use it to weigh down all of the important papers on his or her desk.

Apple Stamp
Paper Bouquet

APPLE STAMP PAPER BOUQUET

Fall is in the air and apples are in season. Create these apple printings and then turn these festive stamps into a beautiful paper bouquet.

Learning Objectives: Children will learn the shape of an apple as they make apple-shaped prints; children will use their imagination as they use apples to represent flowers; children will use fine motor skills as they manipulate the apple to stamp.

SUPPLIES

2 apples, any size or color
Knife (adult only)
4 popsicle sticks
2 oz. bottle of red craft paint
Paper plate
1 sheet of white cardstock paper
Green crayon
Scissors or hole punch
8" piece of red ribbon, ¼" width
12" piece of red ribbon, ¼" width

STEPS

1. You will cut 2 apples to create 4 apple stamps. To give your apple stamps some variety and shape, cut 1 apple in half horizontally straight through the middle and cut the other apple in half vertically, making 4 apple stamps.

2. Insert a popsicle stick into the top side of each apple to use as a handle when you stamp.

3. Next you will make about 5–6 apple stamps on the top center of your white craft paper to form an apple bouquet. Use the photo as a guide. Pour your red craft paint onto a paper plate. Dip an apple stamp into the paint, making sure the cut side of the apple is covered in paint, and stamp it onto the paper. Continue dipping and stamping on your paper until you have about 5–6 stamps in the shape of a bouquet. Let this paint dry.

4. Once the paint is dry, use your crayon to draw a green line from the bottom of each apple stamp to the bottom center of the paper to represent stems on each apple. Make sure each of the green stems reaches the same end point at the bottom middle of the paper, as if this is a bouquet of flowers.

5. With the tip of your scissors, pierce 2 small holes on each side of the gathered green stems (see the photo). This needs to be done by an adult.

6. Lace your 8" ribbon through each hole and tie the ribbon in a knot on the front to make it look like the ribbon is wrapped around a bouquet of flowers.

7. Finally, you will make a hanger for the paper bouquet. Use scissors or a hole punch to make a small hole in each of the top corners of the paper. If using scissors to make your hole, this needs to be done by an adult. Lace your 12" ribbon through one hole and tie it in a knot on the front. Lace the other end of the ribbon through the second hole and tie it in a knot on the front, too.

This bouquet of apple-shaped flowers is ready to hang on your door to celebrate the fall season.

Silly Apple Sandwiches

SILLY APPLE SANDWICHES

These silly apple faces and creatures make for a yummy autumn snack. You can create a child's face or a beloved pet for these silly apple sandwiches.

Learning Objectives: Children will use their creativity and imagination as they craft each apple face; children will use their fine motor skills as they add toppings to make the apple sandwiches.

SUPPLIES

4 apples, any variety
Cutting knife (adult only)
Spreading knife
½ cup miniature marshmallows
½ cup chocolate chips
½ cup raisins
½ cup creamy peanut butter

STEPS

1. Cut 1 apple horizontally into 3–4 round slices. You will use one of these as the base for each sandwich.

2. Cut another apple vertically into 2–3 round slices. You will use these slices to form different parts of the sandwiches.

3. Cut the remaining apples into thin half-circle slices, discarding the center and seeds. You will use these slices to form different parts of the sandwiches.

   Face: Using the photo as a guide, spread a thin layer of peanut butter on one *uncut* side of a circular apple slice. Stick 5–6 marshmallows on the peanut butter to act as hair. Add 2 chocolate chips for eyes, 1 raisin nose, and 1 thin apple slice for a mouth.

   Turtle: Cut 3 of the thin half-circle apple slices in half. Use 5 of the halves to form a star shape on top of a round apple slice (use the photo as a guide); these shapes represent the turtle's arms, legs, and head. Place 1 of the *vertical* apple slices on top of the star shape; this acts as the shell of the turtle (and keeps the star shapes in place). For the turtle's eyes, place a small drop of peanut butter on the center slice of the apple star shape and place 2 chocolate chips on the peanut butter.

   Monster: Spread 2 thin layers of peanut butter at the top of a cut side of a circular apple slice. Stick 2 thin half slices of apple to the peanut butter to act as the monster's horns. Spread a thin layer of peanut butter on the uncut side above the horns. Place 6–8 chocolate chips on the peanut butter for the monster's hair. Place 3 raisins in a row on the apple for eyes. Place 2–3 half slices of apple on the bottom of the apple face to represent the monster's fangs.

These silly sandwiches are going to be a hit with your kids, plus you know they will be eating a healthy snack.

Paper Apple Garland

PAPER APPLE GARLAND

Hang this cheerful apple garland on the mantle or over a doorway to help celebrate the fall season. This banner is simple to create and fun to display.

Learning Objectives: Children will use their creativity while decorating this garland; children will learn an apple's shape; children will use fine motor skills as they cut with scissors.

SUPPLIES

5' piece of yarn, any color
1 sheet of red craft paper
1 sheet of green craft paper
1 sheet of yellow craft paper
1 sheet of brown craft paper
1 green pipe cleaner
Pencil
Craft glue or tape
Scissors

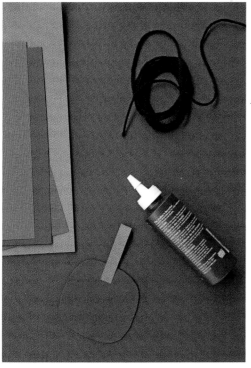

STEPS

1. Draw a 4 × 4" apple shape on your red craft paper. Cut out this apple and use it as a template to cut out 5 more red apples, 6 yellow apples, and 6 green apples (18 total).

2. With your brown paper, cut out 18 stems, 1 × 3" in size for each stem. Glue one end to the top of the apple. Fold the brown stem paper into a loop and glue it down on the other side of the apple. Let the glue dry completely.

3. Thread your yarn through the loop of each apple's stem. You can add a drop of glue or tape to each stem to keep the apple in place on the yarn. Use the main photo as a guide.

4. Cut your green pipe cleaner in half to get 2 pieces. Bend and curl each pipe cleaner piece to create 2 green worms, as shown in the main photo. Place a green worm through the brown stem of one of your apples, which will hold the stem in place. Repeat with the second stem.

Now hang this garland to warm up your home for fall.

OCTOBER

Your house will start to look a little spooky after you make these October projects! Sip your monster milkshake with your pumpkin pal straw or craft a googly eye card for Halloween.

Spook-tacular
Googly Eye Cards

B oo!

I've got my
eyes on you!

BOO!

Sp ooky!

SPOOK-TACULAR GOOGLY EYE CARDS

You can create these spook-tacular Halloween cards with googly eyes, making for eye-popping fun. They are the perfect haunting cards for Halloween.

Learning Objectives: Children will use their creativity as they craft these silly cards; children will use fine motor skills as they cut, color, and glue.

SUPPLIES

1 sheet of orange craft paper, 8½ × 11" size

1 sheet of purple craft paper, 8½ × 11" size

1 sheet of green craft paper, 8½ × 11" size

1 sheet of 8½ × 11" or 12 × 12" decorative craft paper, any color and style

Scissors or paper cutter

Craft glue

14–15 googly eyes, all shapes and sizes

Black marker or crayon

STEPS

Cut the green, orange, and purple craft paper sheets into 5½ × 4¼" sizes each. Fold each paper in half to create a greeting card. Save the extra craft paper from each of the 3 colors to use as accent pieces on each card.

"Spooky!" card: Glue a 4 × 5" piece of decorative paper to your orange card (as shown in the photo). At the bottom of your decorative paper, glue on a 1 × 3" piece of purple paper. Glue 2 large googly eyes next to each another in the center of the purple paper. Write the letters "Sp" on the left side of the googly eyes and the letters "ky" on the right side of the eyes to make the word "Spooky." Use your crayon to add an exclamation mark at the end of "Spooky."

"I've got my eyes on you" card: Glue a 4 × 5" piece of orange craft paper in the center of your green card. Glue a 2 × 3" piece of decorative paper in the center of the orange piece you just glued onto the card. In the center of the decorative paper, glue 10 googly eyes all over, as shown in the photo. On the top of your card, write "I've got my eyes on you!" with a black marker or crayon. Write "BOO!" on the bottom of the card.

"Boo!" card: Glue a 4× 5" piece of decorative paper to your purple card. Glue a 1 × 3" piece of orange paper in the center of your decorative paper, as shown in the photo. On the left side of the orange piece of paper, write the letter "B" with a black marker or crayon. Glue 2 large googly eyes next to the letter B to create the word "BOO." Use your crayon or marker to add an exclamation mark at the end of "BOO."

These creepy eye cards are sure to make your Halloween boo-tastic.

Columbus Day Ship
in a Bottle

COLUMBUS DAY SHIP IN A BOTTLE

You can sail this crafty boat across the ocean as you celebrate the Columbus Day holiday. These miniature boats in a bottle are sure to cross the stormy seas to safety.

Learning Objectives: Children will enhance their science skills as they work with water; children will use their fine motor skills as they create their boat.

SUPPLIES

1- or 2-liter empty plastic bottle, wrapper removed

1 sheet of craft foam, any color

Scissors

1 drinking straw

Magnet, ½"-diameter

Hot glue (adult use only)

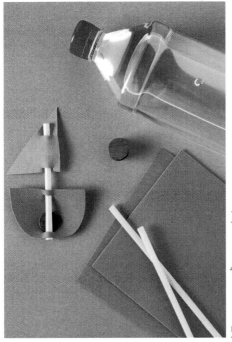

STEPS

1. With your scissors, cut a small 1–2" isosceles right triangle and a 2–3" half circle shape out of your craft foam.

2. Cut 2 small ¼" slits at the top and bottom of the triangle and the half circle, as shown on the diagram.

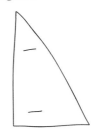

3. With the hot glue gun (adults only), glue your small magnet to the bottom of the half circle, on the curved side. The magnet will help the boat stay upright in the water. Let the glue dry.

4. Thread your straw through the 2 holes of the half circle and then through the 2 holes of the triangle. The craft foam pieces and straw should attach together to form the shape of a sailboat. Trim off any excess straw that is hanging below the bottom of the boat.

5. Fill your plastic bottle halfway with water.

6. Roll your craft foam sailboat into a roll shape and slip it through the opening of the water bottle. It will unroll itself as it moves past the bottle opening.

7. Twist the plastic bottle's lid back on. For a more secure seal on the lid, add some hot glue to the dry lid before you twist it back onto the bottle.

As you move your water bottle around, your ship will be sailing the seven seas. **107**

Pumpkin Straw Pals

PUMPKIN STRAW PALS

On Halloween your little ghosts and goblins can sip their witches' brew from these cute pumpkin straw pals. Or you can use the straws throughout fall for a bit of festive fun throughout the autumn season.

Learning Objectives: Children will learn the colors orange and green, and the shape of a pumpkin; children will enhance their cutting and drawing skills as they create each pumpkin.

SUPPLIES

1 sheet of orange craft paper
1 black marker
Scissors or hole punch
1 green straw (per pumpkin)

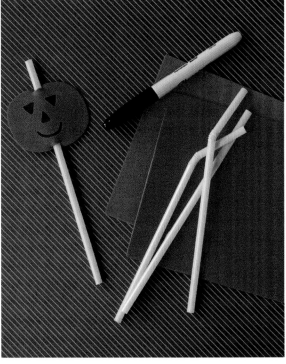

STEPS

1. Cut out a 2–3" pumpkin shape from the orange craft foam. You can make any pumpkin shape you like.

2. Draw a jack-o-lantern face onto the pumpkin shape with your black marker. You can make the face angry or happy, depending on your child's preference.

3. Cut 2 small slits into your pumpkin with your scissors, one at the very top and one at the very bottom, as shown on the diagram. It's easiest to work if you fold your pumpkin in half and cut a ¼" slice at the fold. If you prefer, you can instead use a hole punch to create each hole.

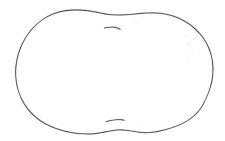

4. Thread your green straw though both of the pumpkin's holes. Let the straw come out at least 1–2" above the top of the pumpkin to represent the stem.

Add this straw to your ghostly beverage glass and start sipping.

Monster
Milkshake

MONSTER MILKSHAKE

Don't let this monster milkshake give you a scare! Sip it up through your red licorice straw before it has the chance to say "Boo"!

Learning Objectives: Children will learn the colors green and purple; children will use their creativity as they make a silly milkshake monster; children will use cooking skills as they work with food.

SUPPLIES

2 cups vanilla ice cream

½ cup milk

Blue, red, and green food coloring

2 small bowls

Blender

1 large clear glass

1 piece of red licorice

2 chocolate cookies

3 orange-colored chocolate-coated candies

STEPS

1. Add 2 cups of vanilla ice cream and ½ cup of milk to your blender and blend until smooth.

2. Pour your milkshake evenly into two bowls. Add 4–5 drops of green food coloring into one bowl. Add 2–3 drops of blue and 2–3 drops of red food coloring into the second bowl to make the milkshake purple.

3. Layer the green-colored ice cream and purple-colored ice cream into the large clear glass, forming stripes of colored ice cream.

4. Cut or bite off the ends of a piece of red licorice. Add it to the center of your glass for the monster's tongue.

5. Crush up your 2 chocolate cookies into a powder and add it to the top of your ice cream for the monster's hair, as shown in the photo.

6. Add 3 orange-colored chocolate-coated candies to the top of the milkshake, under the cookie "hair," to make the monster's eyes. Place the candies in a straight line, as shown in the photo.

Drink up this monster milkshake as fast as you can before it gives you a fright!

NOVEMBER

Your kids will gobble up the pine cone cookies

you make together in November. Or you can

create a few fun sensory activities with the

leaves that are falling off the trees.

Leaf Rubbing
Turkey Feathers

LEAF RUBBING TURKEY FEATHERS

While the children are waiting for Thanksgiving dinner, have them create their own paper turkey. Gather a few leaves from outdoors to help make this turkey come to life.

Learning Objectives: Children will experience science as they create leaf rubbings; children will enhance their hand-eye coordination and fine motor skills as they make each rubbing.

SUPPLIES

5–6 leaves, an assortment of shapes

1 box of crayons

2–3 sheets white printer paper

Scissors

1 sheet of brown craft paper, 8½ × 11" size

2 googly eyes

1 × 1" piece of orange craft paper

1" piece of red pipe cleaner

Craft glue

STEPS

1. Spread out your leaves on a table or hard surface. Next, lay 1 piece of white printer paper over the top of 1 leaf. You will make 5–6 total leaf rubbings, so leave room on your paper to make rubbings of other leaf shapes. Color over the top of the leaf, onto the paper, with a crayon to create a leaf rubbing. You should start to see the shape of the leaf appear on the paper. Make 5–6 more leaf rubbings using different leaf shapes, if you like, and with different crayon colors.

2. With your scissors, cut out each of your leaf rubbings along the outline of the leaf shape.

3. Cut out an 8"-diameter circle from your brown craft paper. This represents the body of the turkey.

4. With a black crayon, draw a 2–3"-diameter circle in the center of your brown paper circle. This represents the turkey's head.

5. Glue 2 googly eyes in the middle of the smaller circle.

6. Cut an isosceles triangle out of your 1 × 1" orange craft paper. This will represent the turkey's beak. Using the photo as a guide, glue this triangular beak under the turkey's eyes.

7. Glue on the red pipe cleaner piece for the turkey's wattle, as shown in the photo.

8. Glue each leaf-rubbing piece onto the rear side of the top of your brown paper circle to form a fan shape (as shown in the photo). The leaf rubbings represent the turkey's feathers.

This turkey is now ready to say, "Gobble, gobble."

Corncob Printing

CORNCOB PRINTING

Create unique-looking paper as you stamp it with an ear of corn. Children can see what will take shape as they discover the touch and feel of this print.

Learning Objectives: Children will gain art skills as they paint; children will learn creativity as they make different painted prints; children will use their senses as they see and feel a different texture.

SUPPLIES

1 corncob
Craft paint, any variety of colors
Paintbrush
1 sheet of craft paper, any color
Newspaper or paper towels

STEPS

1. Brush paint onto your corncob and cover all sides, but leave 1–2" unpainted on each end for handles. You can add layers of paint in a few different colors or just one color. You will hold onto the two ends of the corncob when you paint the craft paper.

2. Lay your painted corncob on one edge of your craft paper. Slowly roll your cob across the paper in one motion. Carefully peel the corncob off the paper and set aside on newspaper or paper towels, or you can paint and roll the cob again.

3. Set the painted picture out to dry. You can always add more paint to your corncob and roll it across the craft paper again. You might want to try rolling your corncob in another direction to create a completely different image.

Let this paper dry completely and then display it for all to see. This stamped paper also makes a great background for other craft projects.

Thankful Crunchy
Leaves Plaque

THANKFUL CRUNCHY LEAVES PLAQUE

Kids will have fun crunching up fallen leaves to create this festive sign. Make this sign to give to a family member or friend, sharing your gratitude during the fall season.

SUPPLIES

10-15 dried leaves

Large bowl

4 × 24" piece of craft wood, ⅛" width

Orange craft paint

Paintbrush

Pencil

White craft glue

STEPS

1. Paint your piece of wood with orange craft paint. Let this dry.
2. Using the photo as a guide, use your pencil to write "THANKFUL" in all capital letters on your painted board. Make sure the letters are evenly spaced across the board.
3. Trace the pencil letters with your white craft glue. Make sure each part of the letters is covered in a line of glue.
4. In a large bowl, crunch up your dried leaves. Try to get them as small as possible.
5. Sprinkle your crushed leaves onto your glue, shaking it around slightly to get each part of the glue covered in leaves. Shake off any excess leaves back into the bowl. Let your board dry overnight.

Now you can display this "thankful" plaque on a shelf, hang it on a wall, or give it to a beloved family member or friend.

Pine Cone
Cookies

PINE CONE COOKIES

These prickly pine cones are just the right treat to snack on when the weather is cold. They make the perfect dessert to eat with your Thanksgiving dinner.

Learning Objectives: Children will use cooking skills as they help you cook in the kitchen; children will use their fine motor skills as they manipulate the chocolate chips.

SUPPLIES

1 roll of pre-made sugar cookie dough

Butter knife or plastic knife

Oval-shaped cookie cutter (optional)

Cookie sheet

1 package of pre-made chocolate frosting

12 oz. bag of milk chocolate chips

STEPS

1. Preheat your oven to the temperature listed on the sugar cookie directions.
2. Roll out your cookie dough to ¼" thick.
3. Use your butter knife or plastic knife to cut an oval that resembles the shape of a pine cone and place on a cookie sheet. Using a butter knife will give the edge of your pine cone cookie a more rustic look. You can also use an oval-shaped cookie cutter if you prefer. Continue making pine cone shapes with all of the remaining dough.
4. Bake your cookies according to the package or recipe directions and let them cool.
5. Frost each cookie with chocolate frosting.
6. Add chocolate chips to the top of the cookies by laying them on their sides to represent the pokey parts of a pine cone. Space the chips evenly in small rows, filling the whole cookie.

These pine cone cookies are ready to plate up and eat for a prickly treat.

DECEMBER

December is all about traditions and this

chapter has a few fun projects to help you

celebrate the holiday season. Get ready to

light pretend candles and trim a paper tree.

Stained Glass
Paper Menorah

STAINED GLASS PAPER MENORAH

Hang this stained glass paper menorah near a window to watch the colorful candles come to life. Display it for all to see during the eight nights of Hanukkah.

Learning Objectives: Children will see how light passes through colored tissue paper to create a stained-glass-window effect; children will use their fine motor skills as they fold and cut the paper.

SUPPLIES

1 sheet of 8½ × 11" cardstock paper, any color

Pencil

Ruler

Scissors

1 sheet yellow tissue paper

4 sheets of tissue paper in a variety of colors

Craft glue

STEPS

1. With a pencil and ruler, draw 9 evenly spaced vertical lines, about 1–2" apart, across your cardstock paper. Use the photo as a guide.

2. Fold your paper on each of the 9 marked lines.

3. About 2" up on the first fold, make a small ⅛" horizontal cut. Measure up 4" from the first cut and make a second ⅛" horizontal cut into the same fold. Now cut from the bottom cut to the top cut, forming a long rectangle when the paper is unfolded.

4. About ½" above the cut-out rectangle, cut out a crescent shape from the fold. This crescent-shaped cut will form an oval shape when you unfold the paper, as shown in the photo.

5. Repeat steps 3 and 4 for each of the remaining 8 folds. You can cut the middle rectangle candle 1" longer than the rest of the candles in order to help it stand out.

6. Open up your paper and lay it flat. On the backside of the paper, glue yellow tissue paper over the 9 oval-shaped holes, but don't cover the rectangular-shaped cutouts.

7. Glue 9 strips of colored tissue paper over the 9 cut-out rectangles, alternating colors as shown in the photo. Let the glue dry.

Hold up your paper to a window and you'll see the bright colors come through, creating a stained glass menorah.

Oat Cereal
Wreaths

OAT CEREAL WREATHS

You can make these crunchy-munchy wreath treats during the Christmas season. These oat wreaths are fun and festive, and are the perfect project for little hands to help with in the kitchen.

Learning Objectives: Children will learn science skills as they cook in the kitchen; children will learn math skills as they help with measuring the ingredients; children will work on fine motor skills as they manipulate food.

SUPPLIES

5 cups toasted-oat cereal
½ cup butter
4 cups marshmallows
Large saucepan
Tray
Butter knife
Wax paper
1 green gumdrop (per wreath)
3 red candy-coated chocolate pieces (per wreath)

STEPS

1. In a large saucepan, melt the butter and marshmallows on low heat until melted together. Take off the heat and mix in your toasted-oat cereal.
2. Pour the oat-cereal mix onto wax paper and let it cool.
3. Once cooled, pull off a handful of mix. (You may want to spray cooking spray on your hands to keep the marshmallow mix from sticking to your hands.) Form it into a 4 × 4" wreath shape with a hole in the center and place on a tray. Continue to pull off handfuls of mix and shape them into wreaths until all the mix is used.
4. To make the berries, place 3 red candy-coated chocolate pieces around the top of each wreath and press it in slightly. Use the photo as guide.
5. To make the holly leaves, cut 1 green gumdrop in half with your butter knife and place 1 piece on each side of the red candy piece on the bottom of the wreath. Press in slightly to make sure the gumdrops stick to the wreath. Add gumdrop leaves to all the remaining wreaths.

Place these wreaths on a platter and serve at your next holiday gathering.

Candy Cane
Headband Antlers

CANDY CANE HEADBAND ANTLERS

With these candy cane reindeer antlers, your kids can help lead Santa's sleigh this Christmas. Your children can get silly and playful when they pretend they are one of Santa's reindeer.

Learning Objectives: Children will use their fine motor skills as they twist the pipe cleaners and wrap the ribbon around the headband; children will pretend play as they become a reindeer.

SUPPLIES

1 plastic headband, new or used
6' piece of brown ribbon,
    ⅝" width
Craft glue
2 white pipe cleaners
2 red pipe cleaners

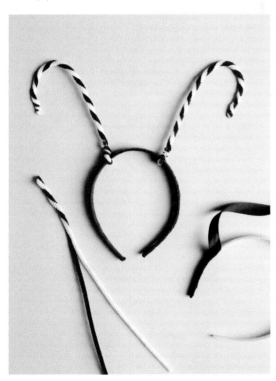

STEPS

1. Glue one end of the ribbon to one end of the headband. Wrap the ribbon around and around the headband, overlapping each wrap, until the entire headband is covered in ribbon. Add glue to the back of the ribbon at the end to attach it. Let the glue dry completely.

2. For the antlers, twist together 1 red pipe cleaner with 1 white pipe cleaner. Do the same thing with the remaining red and white pipe cleaners. Bend each twisted pipe cleaner into a candy-cane shape.

3. To attach the antlers to the headband, bend 1–2" of the bottom of one candy cane pipe cleaner around the headband and about 1–2" away from the center. Twist the pipe cleaner together with itself as you secure it around the headband. Repeat this step for the second candy-cane pipe cleaner, but place it 3–4" away from the first pipe cleaner so that both candy canes look like antlers, as shown in the photo.

Your children can enjoy the Christmas season as they pretend that they're Santa's reindeer.

Paper Spiral Christmas
Tree Mobile

PAPER SPIRAL CHRISTMAS TREE MOBILE

This is the perfect Christmas tree for children to create. Hang this spiral Christmas tree mobile in your home and watch it spin in place.

Learning Objectives: Children will develop their cutting skills and learn a spiral shape as they create this spiral tree; children will use their fine motor skills as they glue on each bead ornament.

SUPPLIES

1 sheet green cardstock paper, 8½ × 11" size

Pencil

Scissors

Hole punch

10" piece of yellow ribbon, any width

10 red plastic pony beads

10 white plastic pony beads

Craft glue

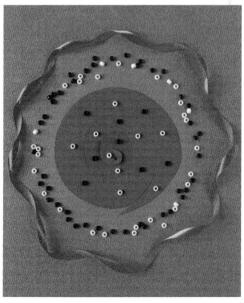

STEPS

1. With your pencil, draw a spiral pattern like the one shown here onto your green cardstock paper. Start the spiral at the *edge* of your paper and go in a circle 2–3" around from the next line, all the way up to the center of the paper.

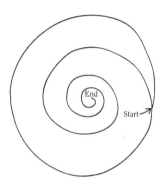

2. Cut out the spiral pattern along the pencil lines with your scissors. Trim the edges if you need to give it a smooth look. If you hold up the center of the spiral, it should look like a "falling" spiral Christmas tree.

3. Use the hole punch to punch a hole in the top of your hanging spiral. Thread your yellow ribbon through the hole and tie it in a knot on the underside of the hole.

4. Glue your red and white plastic beads onto the paper all the way around the spiral. These beads represent the ornaments on your spiral Christmas tree. Let the glue dry completely.

Find the perfect spot to hang your new paper spiral Christmas tree and it's sure to bring you holiday cheer.

Kwanzaa Pipe Cleaner
Candleholder

KWANZAA PIPE CLEANER CANDLEHOLDER

Create this kid-friendly *kinara* (a Swahili word meaning "candleholder") that is perfect for celebrating Kwanzaa. Add one pipe cleaner candle for each of the seven nights of Kwanzaa.

Learning Objectives: Children will work with the colors black, red, green, and yellow; children will use their fine motor skills as they twist each pipe cleaner in a shape that looks like a candle.

SUPPLIES

4–5"-diameter smooth foam disc

Black craft paint

1 small paper plate

Paintbrush

3 red pipe cleaners

3 green pipe cleaners

1 black pipe cleaner

2 yellow pipe cleaners

Scissors

STEPS

1. Pour some black craft paint on the paper plate and then use your paintbrush to paint the entire foam disc black. Let this dry completely. This serves as the base of the candleholder.

2. Cut each yellow pipe cleaner into fourths. You will need 7 of the small pieces.

3. Fold 1 of the red pipe cleaners in half. Fold 1 yellow piece of pipe cleaner in half. Lay the small folded yellow piece on top of and in the middle of the red folded pipe cleaner, as shown in the first diagram. Bend the yellow pipe cleaner around the red pipe cleaner as you fold the yellow pipe cleaner in half again. Now fold the red pipe cleaner in half again, as shown in the second diagram.

4. Using the third diagram as a guide, twist the red folded pipe cleaner to itself as well as the yellow pipe cleaner to itself. This creates a red candle with a yellow flame.

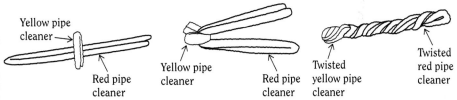

Yellow pipe cleaner · Red pipe cleaner · Yellow pipe cleaner · Red pipe cleaner · Twisted yellow pipe cleaner · Twisted red pipe cleaner

5. Repeat steps 3 and 4 with the remaining red, green, and black pipe cleaners. You will end up with 3 red candles, 3 yellow candles, and 1 black candle.

6. Once you have made all 7 candles, press each pipe cleaner candle in the black foam disc a few inches apart. Use the photo as a guide for placement of the candles. The candles should press in easily.

Now your kinara is ready to display for Kwanzaa.

LEARNING WHILE CRAFTING: A LEARNING OBJECTIVES OVERVIEW

Crafting is not only fun for children, it is also a learning opportunity. As you create the projects in this book together, your child will also be learning—improving his or her fine and gross motor skills as well as hand-eye coordination, problem solving, even doing a bit of math. Learning objectives are listed for each craft project in this book so you know what you can expect your child to be learning as he or she crafts a particular project. A few of the most commonly referenced objectives are explained below in further detail.

- **Hand-eye Coordination:** Hand-eye coordination involves the action of a child using his or her hands in coordination with his or her eyes to perform a skill. Tasks such as threading a piece of yarn through the large hole of a bead and decorating a cookie with frosting or candies are examples of using hand-eye coordination.
- **Motor Skills:**
    Fine (or small) motor skills: Fine motor skills involve using one's hands and fingers. Most of the craft projects in this book develop a child's fine motor skills. Tasks such as wrapping ribbon, gluing beads onto a project, threading yarn, or coloring with crayons all utilize a child's fine motor skills.
    Gross (or large) motor skills: Gross motor skills focus on the larger movements that a child makes, such as tossing a bean bag, rolling a ball, or even jumping and running.
- **Recognition:** As they create the projects in this book, children can enhance their recognition of things around them, learning to recognize letters, shapes, or colors by performing a particular activity.
- **Pretend Play:** When children engage in pretend play—pretending to become something or someone different, acting out in dramatic play with figurines or as a character—they are enhancing their social skills, language skills, thinking skills, and imagination. Children might pretend play in a play kitchen setting, with small sea creature figurines, or by trying on a silly reindeer headband.

ABOUT THE AUTHOR

Marie LeBaron lives in the Pacific Northwest and is a wife and mother to three beautiful children. She graduated with an Early Childhood and Elementary Education teaching degree and taught kindergarten for several years. She now shares many of the tips and tricks she's learned over the years on her blog, Make and Takes. Always having a love of crafts, she enjoys getting messy with glue and glitter. There's always some sort of project going on and her kitchen counter is often cluttered with crafts. When she's not making and taking with her kids, she loves to read, run, and blog!